Poésies
and complete miscellanea

Also by
Alexis Lykiard:

Novels:
The Summer Ghosts
Zones
A Sleeping Partner
Strange Alphabet
The Stump
Instrument of Pleasure
Last Throes
The Drive North

Poetry:
Robe of Skin
Greek Images
Eight Lovesongs
Lifelines
Milesian Fables

Translation:
Lautréamont's Maldoror

Poésies

**and complete miscellanea by
Isidore Ducasse
also known as**

Lautréamont

*with English and French texts
edited and translated by*
Alexis Lykiard

Allison & Busby
London and New York

First published in Britain 1978 by
Allison & Busby Limited, 6a Noel Street,
London W1V 3RB

Reprinted 1980

Distributed in the U.S.A. by
Schocken Books Inc., 200 Madison Avenue,
New York, NY10016

Translation, preface,
notes, bibliography and additional material
copyright © 1978 Alexis Lykiard

ISBN 0 85031 238 8
ISBN 0 85031 239 6 Pbk

Printed in Great Britain by
A. Wheaton & Company Limited,
Exeter

This book has been
published with financial assistance from
the Arts Council of Great Britain

Contents

Preface without memoirs
7

A Ducasse chronology
23

Poésies I
28

Poésies II
55

Notes to Poésies
92

Letters
117

Notes to Letters
130

Apocrypha
133

Notes to Apocrypha
135

Biographical reminiscences of Isidore Ducasse
136

Contemporary reactions to Lautréamont
145

Bibliography
148

Addenda
151

Preface Without Memoirs

1.
Re-Creations

... The poem demands the demise of the poet who writes it and the birth of the poet who reads it.
  (Octavio Paz: *Alternating Current*)

On the twenty-fourth of November 1870 Edmond de Goncourt noted in his *Journal* that "the rag-picker of our boulevard, who at the moment keeps a place in the queue at the market for a low eating-house keeper," had told a servant "that he was buying, for his employer, cats at six francs, rats at one franc, and dog-flesh at one franc fifty, the pound". Also that morning, at his lodgings not far off – a modest hotel, 7 Faubourg-Montmartre – the almost unknown pseudonymous author of an extraordinary, unread masterpiece of black humour (in which a ragman appears as one of the few disinterestedly charitable characters) died from unascertained causes aged only twenty-four.

It was the strange destiny of Isidore Ducasse to be born in curious domestic circumstances whose precise details are lacking, in one capital city under siege – Montevideo – and to die very young, thousands of miles away in another capital city under siege – Paris, where his death certificate baldly stated *sans autres renseignements*. Of such ironies, coincidences and ambiguous phrases are legends made. It is not the purpose of this Preface to add to the biographical inventions and speculation through which Ducasse's brief life has been re-created and indeed distorted for more than a century. Readers who wish to know the facts about Ducasse's life, meagre though these facts may be, are referred to the Chronology on pp.23-7. There has been one indispensable biography, impeccably researched and documented, lucidly written: *Isidore Ducasse, Comte de Lautréamont* (Paris, Editions de la Table Ronde, 1970), by François Caradec, to whom all those interested in Ducasse and his work must be grateful. But the last fifteen years have, not altogether surprisingly, witnessed the expansion of the Lautréamont industry too: a mass of shamelessly inflated books, academic and otherwise, inspired by myth-making necrophilia, blind adulation, or a pedan-

tic desire to debunk or dissect (the various authors being unable actually to exhume, through ignorance of their exact resting place, Ducasse's mortal remains) a controversial and thus still fresh body of work, in quasi-Surrealist terms an exquisite corpus.

The odour of humourless reverence surrounding so much Ducassian criticism ought, I believe, to be dispelled, along with the glib dismissals of his work by the staid establishment factions who ignored it then as they continue to do now. With this in mind, my opening paragraph and the first sentence of the next, while valid statements containing no untruths, are intended as examples of the "literary-detection" style, the popularising bait on the bookmaker's hook. This attention-grabbing device, of which the author of *Les Chants de Maldoror* (especially in *Chant* 6) was so well aware, he himself celebrated and exposed simultaneously. The point I want to make is that all his work – and herein lies much of its originality – contains its own built-in criticism, and that this criticism, too, continually varies its approach. Ducasse's jokes, in fact, reveal their underlying deadly seriousness to the reader via that reader's own awareness of style and sensitivity to tone. Of course, to mix genres, to deal in paradox and parody and make abrupt transitions whether thematic or stylistic, ensures a stimulating and multi-faceted, rather than an easy or easily classifiable, read.

It also explains some of the enduring fascination of Lautréamont-Ducasse (whose very choice of titles and proper names is significantly paradoxical and is examined in the second section of this Preface) and why a literary historian as eminent as Mario Praz in *The Romantic Agony* (1933) – a very long book indeed in which one would expect "our" author to be of central importance – consigns *Les Chants de Maldoror* to the tail-end of a chapter, allotting it just one almost apologetic page and some footnotes and ignoring the *Poésies* altogether. Postwar editions included no revisions or expansions of his original judgements that the *Chants* were "a late but extreme case of cannibalistic Byronism" and their author "a macabre humourist in whom it is impossible to distinguish where sincerity ends and mystification begins".

But both these comments, though inadequate, are well worth examining. The only cannibalism as such in the *Chants* is that of God preying upon man – one reason why Maldoror their eponymous hero (*mal d'aurore*, or dawn's evil, as one commentator suggests) opposes the Deity and indeed all authority that cramps the spirit. If Praz meant Lautréamont's *own* cannibalism (the insertion and assimilation within the *Chants* of items based on contemporary news and whole passages transcribed from Dr Chenu's *Encyclopedia of Natural History*, for in-

stance, not to mention many very conscious echoes, borrowings and reworkings from sources as diverse as Dante, Homer, Shakespeare, the Bible, Maturin, Baudelaire and Sue) he was quite correct. Even more so, in a sense, if referring to autophagy – for Ducasse more emphatically than most writers lived *in* and *for* books, drew material from them, expressing himself through them, consuming himself and becoming his work, remaining otherwise memoir-less, faceless and anonymous both by intention and, finally, accident. Praz (again, whether by intention or accident) was touching on subjects that have become crucial to Lautréamont studies. Peter Nesselroth in *Lautréamont's Imagery* puts it thus: "The poet . . . incorporates into the text, into the creation of his own personality (since Lautréamont is non-existent, an assumed name taken from a fictional character), the world around him: plagiarisms, literary precedents, his own judgements on what he has just written, the reader, etc. The text is inclusive and must of necessity be discontinuous." This sort of technical experimentation did not really fit Praz's thesis, so, faced with what Roger Caillois called "a work which contains its own commentary", he tried to label and dismiss it simultaneously, resorting to talk of "sincerity" and "mystification", moralising generalities here irrelevant, for as Octavio Paz says, "the writer's morality does not lie in the subjects he deals with or the arguments he sets forth, but in his behaviour towards language."

All Lautréamont-Ducasse's work is consistent: it explores the different possibilities and limitations of fiction, of literature as artefact. *Les Chants de Maldoror* and the *Poésies* are different approaches to the alchemy of the word. When we read in *Les Chants*, "I know that my annihilation will be complete," it is as if death is seen as illegibility, oblivion being the state beyond language and words: words are our very life, and in the beginning was the Word, Word as Life. If our culture too is rooted in language, and that culture is unsatisfactory or the time has come to reshape it, we must first attack language and remake that. Which is what Ducasse, singlehanded, ambitiously and in some ways suicidally, tried to do. By means of what Francis Ponge called the "*Maldoror-Poésies* apparatus" Ducasse sought to demonstrate and explore new ways of reading and writing, and it is how he did it that makes him so important to both writers and readers today.

2.
Names and Titles

Words are very much like lizards; they change colour according to position.

(Lafcadio Hearn: *Talks to Writers*)

... language is a sort of transformation mechanism: the different combinations of words – that is to say, their position within the phrase – produce meaning. This phenomenon is repeated again on the level of the text: the meaning varies according to the position of the sentences.

(Octavio Paz: *Alternating Current*)

Ducasse's ambiguities, mystifications, wordgames – labels themselves implying different degrees of interest or support granted by reader to author – begin at the very beginning, with names and titles. What are we to make of *Chants*, songs that are not songs, the word implying "canto", "lay", "epic", leading us in turn to expect conventional modes of storytelling, narratives of a certain musicality. Instead, we find mixed genres, prose-poetry and poetic prose, the Gothic fantasy, the serial novel, horror and humour, authorial interventions, disruptions of space and time, stories-within-stories, plagiarisms, techniques of collage, changes of style as frequent as the ubiquitous Maldoror's own metamorphoses, and an elliptical rather than linear structure. The name Maldoror, suggesting as it does evil, gold, horror, dawn, sadness etc, seems a curious hybrid, but on reading the work its full title, *Les Chants de Maldoror par Le Comte de Lautréamont*, seems to contain and imply the constant switches in narrative emphasis – the self as a game (je-*jeu*) and the author as observer, participant and invisible man – as well as being an inevitable and accurate condensation of, or hint at, the contents. And these particular pieces are both popular (in the sense that many of their props belong to the romantic and serial fictions then in vogue) and esoteric (in that the apparently familiar surface meanings are always being questioned if not undermined on deeper levels). These "songs" do not comfort or flow along mindlessly: they herald a black lyricism of the future that will influence twentieth-century literature, through Surrealism, via Céline and Genet – a note also sounded by Kafka, Henry Miller, Beckett, Burroughs and many others since. As Artaud recognised, "if the Maldoror pose is acceptable in a book, it is acceptable only after the poet's death – maybe a hundred years later – when the astringent explosives of the poet's virid heart have had time to calm down",

while for Octavio Paz, Lautréamont is "the poet who discovered the *form* in which to express psychic explosion".

The risk-taking originality of such a controversial book (and discussions about blasphemy and obscenity are the least of the controversies it has aroused), coming at a time when in France Romanticism as a movement seemed outworn if not dead, when war and revolutions were commonplace and yet so often inconclusive, and when politics were sterile and unsettled with the established order – the Second Empire – falling apart, ensured that it would encounter the predictable reactions: a history of censorship problems and clandestinity, of incomprehension and scarcely any sales or reviews.

It might, too, have caused personal offence. When the first *Chant* was published – separately and anonymously – by Balitout, Questroy et Cie, Paris, in August 1868, and subsequently reprinted at Bordeaux in Evariste Carrance's anthology *Parfums de l'Ame* in January 1869, it contained various specific references to Georges Dazet, one of Ducasse's former schoolmates and a dedicatee of the later *Poésies*. When the *Chants* were all published together in book form these references were deleted, the name Dazet metamorphosed into various rather unappealing creatures – octopus, toad, vampire bat and so on. We do not know whether these deletions were on artistic grounds (certainly the book version is the more successful) or because Ducasse or the publishers feared they were libellous.

In these circumstances a pseudonym was a wise decision. But when we look at the actual choice of name, further conjecture seems inevitable. Does this self-conferred nobility, *Comte* de Lautréamont, purposely link the writer with the Marquis de Sade and Lord Byron in an aristocratic élite of the intellect? A symbolic trinity perhaps, of men in many senses superior to their own societies, yet forced beyond the pales of those societies. Sinners who defied God and social taboos, who despised their own fame and infamy alike with patrician detachment or scathing wit. And that other sympathetic failure and aristocrat, the Marquis de Vauvenargues, "corrected" in the *Poésies*, had died as Ducasse himself would, young, poor and unread in Paris leaving, like him, no portrait other than his work. . . . Or was it yet another antibourgeois joke – that to be well-read, in both senses, a title couldn't be bad, might even be *necessary*?

As for "Lautréamont", Latréaumont was Eugene Sue's hero in the novel of that title published in 1838. Was this clear homage to Sue, whose work we know Ducasse had read? Or is the slightly altered name merely a joke on Ducasse's part: i.e. readers be warned, do not expect a straightforward school-of-Eugene-Sue novel? Hubert Juin, with Maurice

Saillet one of the few really excellent editor-critics of Ducasse, notes that the name appears nowhere except on the first, Lacroix edition (anyhow printed in Belgium); and that there is no explanation or mention of it in the Letters. Nor, of course, is there a manuscript of *Les Chants de Maldoror* against which to check. Could the displaced *u* then be a printer's error that has itself entered the fiction, become a mythprint? Others have read into the name anagrammatic references to such as Amon-Ra (the Egyptian god) and ingenious coded jokes by Ducasse: he was printing the book with the allowance sent by his father, to whom it would almost certainly not appeal; hence, a sardonic reference – *Le com/p/te* (the account/bill) – *est à l'autre, à Mont/evideo*!

Ducasse only put his own name to the *Poésies*, which are not, naturally, poems at all but prose – gnomic comments and maxims from Pascal, Vauvenargues and others, juxtaposed without explanation or notes, as if to disconcert the reader with preconceptions still more thoroughly. This material is then turned into a collage of new aphorisms with a new logic of their own, in an attempt to sweep away many stale ideas and clichés and evolve a new kind of writing in the process. By implication a whole bourgeois culture based on tradition, on neat literary pigeonholes within which false polarities like "classic" and "romantic" can be contained, and upon the concept of literary ownership, is threatened. Is plagiarism proper? Is it valid as procedure? And what is plagiarism anyhow? Who owns what? How does an author own his work? Buyers of the *Poésies* were urged to pay what they liked, but not to refuse to accept the booklets, which themselves originally appeared as two small brochures, neither book nor magazine – thus raising further questions about form and content. Are the *Poésies* to be regarded as the "correction" of *Les Chants de Maldoror*, a sort of moral antidote, as Ducasse maintains in his correspondence, or was this assertion also a tongue-in-cheek ploy to extract extra funds from suspicious bankers and to impress publishers like Verboeckhoven? His tone keeps changing as he declares his intention to sing of good as opposed to the "evil" *Chants*: perhaps the lofty, impressive-sounding *Poésies* implies a different kind of morality, an opposition to merely pragmatic prose. Is it the preface to a longer work-in-progress, as suggested, or a final renunciation of fiction in general and of its romantic and classical forms in particular? In relation to the *Chants* are the *Poésies* conversion, reversal, denial, logical progression, the other half of a dialectic, temporary footnote or last word? The author, Isidore Ducasse, is also the editor, I.D., of this ephemeral periodical that through publication in book form has now become permanent. Who really is the author, what is his identity and relationship to the reader? Is the author himself a fiction,

an idea (*idée* and I.D. have the same French pronunciation) in the reader's mind? *"Si j'existe,"* he wrote, *"je ne suis pas un autre,"* yet Ducasse as author is elusive, a chameleon altering colour as swiftly as his words, Whitmanically contradicting himself and containing multitudes. Evidently recalling "My name is Legion, for we are many", a medical man like Dr Soulier has, in all sanity, produced a whole book, *Lautréamont Génie ou Maladie Mentale* (Geneva, Droz, 1964) devoted to proving that Ducasse was mad. At any rate, when reading *Les Chants de Maldoror* by Lautréamont and the *Poésies* by Ducasse we should be aware of the different literary personae and tactics employed without necessarily diagnosing schizophrenia. Researchers delving into the life or the works or both will find that the only ultimate certainty is that interpretations, like the texts themselves, lead to infinity. Perhaps that is the only "meaning" to be drawn from the labyrinth of Lautréamont, the *dédales* of Ducasse.

Finally, it may be salutary to recollect what Kenneth Rexroth wrote in *An Autobiographical Novel*: "For a while I used pseudonyms – the only one which I remember was 'J. Rand Talbot'. There is no reason in the world why I did this except that I was fifteen years old and thought writers should have pen names."

3.
Letters and Critics

... the magnetic extravagance of his letters, those dark iron-fisted dictates he sent with such elegance – cordiality, even.... Extravagant? Of course. Those letters have that harsh extravagance of a man who rushes forward with his lyricism like an erect avenging blade in one hand or the other....

(Antonin Artaud: *Letter on Lautréamont*)

Seeking a writer's identity, biographers try to catch that writer off-guard, looking for revelations of intimacy, personal glimpses, casual remarks made to friends. Ducasse presents further problems: he had so few friends, despite the yearning emphasis upon friendship throughout his work, despite "As long as my friends do not die, I shall not speak of death" (*Poésies* II) – and his isolation in Paris is confirmed by the mere handful of letters that survive, none of them to friends. Acquaintances

and associates, such as the journalists Sircos and Damé (see *Poésies* Note 1) were Parisians anyhow, easily accessible.

So what is to be gleaned from the Letters? The impression of a certain caustic impatience, curious and furious phraseology, macabre humour: all this can be found in his published works too. Yet in the belligerent tone of the Letters there is an appealing rawness, a *naïveté* along with the self-confidence. Although his work is "vanity-published" and he has little if any experience of the literary rat-race, he knows what he is doing. Convinced of his own merit, his arrogance is balanced out by anxiety, that anxiety he shares with most authors who want to see their work published, reviewed, recognised — at least to provoke some reaction other than delay and silence. Probably through hurt pride he feigns Olympian indifference, lack of interest. To Darasse the banker he writes in a different tone, discussing the new direction his writing is taking but probably only in order to convince Darasse of his reliability, whatever his father may have said. What a strange way, however, for a remittance man to reassure the banker in charge of those paternal payments from Uruguay!

Valéry Larbaud even saw the *Poésies* as a book fabricated for M. François Ducasse's benefit — to show him that his son was working, that the morbidity of *Maldoror* and its contemptuous references to greybeards and patriarchal authority in general had given way to something more . . . wholesome. Ducasse's one and only return visit home to Montevideo, in 1867, was, considering the long and hazardous ocean journey involved and the fact that he had been away at school in France for so many years, short indeed — and may have been cut shorter by disagreements. Ducasse the established civil servant had probably (from the existing evidence) been party to a social cover-up when his young wife committed suicide so soon after her son's birth, and had ensured that the documents relating to her death were misleading and vague and that her grave was unmarked. (It remains untraceable to this day.) This Ducasse, Ducasse *père*, the respectable public official, would scarcely have thought too highly of a bizarre young stranger, returning like a prodigal after scant educational success. Exams either not taken or not passed. Isidore's manner sardonic, his lack of respect marked. . . . However, it is all too easy to fill in the fascinating lacunae, to point up the paradoxes: such speculation is conjectural, as Larbaud himself must have been aware when advancing what remains just another possibility, an interesting theory or angle. I find it unconvincing: Isidore Ducasse was too conscious a writer not to know that the book and its methods would be misunderstood, even ignored, just as *Maldoror* had been. One pays a price for innovation, and innovators, knowing this, are hardly

conciliators: books are not written specifically to please others; they are written, like it or not, to please oneself – and Montevideo and his father must have seemed, on Isidore's return to Paris, even further away.

Edmond Jaloux, in his perceptive 1938 Preface to the Corti edition of the *Oeuvres Complètes*, seems to me much nearer the point when sensibly insisting on the fact of Ducasse's own youth: the letters of young people are filled with posturing and however earnest or apparently sincere at the time of writing are not holy writ, nor mature, permanent statements of belief or intent, based as they inevitably are upon inexperience. Thus it is preferable to regard the Letters as tactical rather than as expressions of Ducasse's long-term policy or as forming any kind of definitive credo about his work or methods. They are fascinating fragments to be sure: but we do not know what response they aroused in their recipients, and we should remember that Ducasse himself wrote: "Criticism must attack the form, never the content of your ideas, of your language." Epistolary form, almost more than any other, is of necessity temporary and incomplete, time's prisoner, as books are not. It is to the books one must return therefore, and, inevitably if reluctantly, to the critics, because critical responses to Lautréamont have been so plentiful and so confusing, so misguided and so illuminating, and because his work more than most demands explication, dealing as it does with so many crucial ways of writing *and* reading a book. To outline however briefly some of the points raised by *Les Chants de Maldoror* and *Poésies* and developed or appropriated by the different critical schools of thought may be of use to readers now faced with this first complete annotated edition of the *Poésies* to appear in English.

It must be said that Ducasse's style in both *Les Chants de Maldoror* and *Poésies* would not endear him, in any century, to Academe. As a widely read, deeply serious intellectual he would appear to be that "literary" writer beloved of academic critics, but then he slips through the net, evades categorisation even more emphatically because of *how* he writes than what he says. In the *Poésies* as in the *Chants* Ducasse will treat the reader sometimes as an accomplice, making him do the work of re-establishing or supplying missing links; on other occasions the reader is treated like a child faced with an omnipotent teacher – the author – who yet again is adopting an ironic, tongue-in-cheek metamorphosis. Sly jokes harnessed to or emanating from, deadpan seriousness. The conventions are not being observed, and such breaches threaten critical strongholds! Critics need categories: their bread and butter depends on their dictating fashions, founding Movements, and generally deciding which books are readable (prescribed) and unreadable (proscribed).

There is very little easily available or reliable criticism of Lautréamont in English (see my Bibliographies to *Lautréamont's Maldoror* and this edition) and the "official" or textbook approach is best summed up by this extract from *French Literature and Its Background 5: The Late Nineteenth Century* (Oxford University Press, 1969) — the only fleeting mention of Lautréamont in 229 pages: "Hugo visualised the poet as a giant with his head in the clouds. Rimbaud, Nerval, and possibly Lautréamont are also vivid examples of this barely literary position: they appeared, through semi-madness or a state of quasi-hypnotic enthusiasm, to have 'jumped' the process of metaphoric analogy, and experienced directly, in hallucinations and dreams, incursions of real life into the Ideal. The subsequent image of madman/genius can only appear to an idealist such as Mallarmé as an utter misconception." Bully for Mallarmé and academic caution. The cosy brush-off, the misleading bedfellows, all lunatics together!

Mention of mental instability leads us to the views of Léon Bloy and others, a chiefly French school of thought which we may call the Analysts. This group brand Ducasse the mad genius, and its adherents include the aforementioned Dr Soulier producing entire books diagnosing paranoid schizophrenia in Ducasse. An overlapping group is that of the Biographers, who cogitate, often at inordinate length, like Edouard Peyrouzet, on Ducasse's life, the effect being one of building bricks without straw and unverifiable if occasionally interesting hypotheses. Facts and particulars concerning Ducasse are especially hard to come by, and assiduous researchers in Montevideo and the Tarbes area are needed more urgently than hyper-imaginative biographers, as only M. Caradec, who has written the one valuable full-scale biography of Ducasse to date, has realised.*

There are the Religious Apologists, who interpret *Les Chants de Maldoror* in the light of a struggle between God and the Devil, interesting themselves in Biblical references, visions of the Apocalypse, and any links with Milton, Dante, Blake, etc. Léon-Pierre Quint was one of the earliest and best of these critics, whom the Surrealists, the next school,

---

*The very week these words were written, with this edition on its way to press, exciting news in *La Quinzaine Littéraire*, no.264 (1-15 October 1977), of the rediscovery of the only known photograph (hitherto presumed entirely lost) of Isidore Ducasse, by a young researcher from Tarbes, Jacques Lefrère, who includes it in his important new book, *Le Visage de Lautréamont* (Paris, Pierre Horay, 1977). We reproduce it on the cover by kind permission of the publishers.

often scornfully dismissed, for as Alquié states in *The Philosophy of Surrealism*, "Surrealism charges the idea of God with limiting man, of hindering him from essaying the conquest of all his powers. This is no satanism, but humanist confidence . . .". For the Surrealists anyway, Lautréamont was a kind of sacred ancestor: he had after all been rediscovered, reprinted and extolled by Breton, Soupault, Aragon and co., interpreted as oracle, precursor of their movement, and was sweepingly adopted as authority for the use of random imagery – the famous *beau comme* series in *Les Chants de Maldoror*, the chance meeting on a dissection table of sewing machine and umbrella, etc. – and for automatic writing, although it is doubtful if a work as complex as the *Chants* could have been written at great speed.

The Surrealists begat further progeny, such as the Myth- and Symbol-Hunters, among them the interesting Bachelard (Lautréamont's bestiary) and that indefatigable double-act Mezei and Jean, who plumb the hermetic depths of Jung, the cabbala and alchemy, managing simultaneously to be speculative and dogmatic. The Philosophers (usually Procrustean) include Camus, who could not make the Lautréamont of the *Chants* fit his thesis in *L'Homme Revolté* and therefore patronised the Ducasse of the *Poésies* ("laborious banalities"), and Georges Bataille, who in his book *Literature and Evil* (in which Lautréamont is an obvious omission), probably because of his bitter defection from Breton and followers, evades the issue altogether in an awkward footnote. Oddly enough, the Camus book's English edition, *The Rebel* (Penguin), completely omits the section on Ducasse! Which leads us to the Omitters, Excluders and Dismissers, men like Mario Praz and academic literary historians such as those in the Oxford University Press publication mentioned earlier: these critics and their guided tours are themselves set to rights and supplemented by the Thesis-Makers and Bibliographers. Excellent pioneering work has been done in this field by the likes of Pierre Capretz, Paul Zweig, Frans de Haes, P-O. Walzer and Nesselroth – the latter also appearing under the last and to date most stimulating category, that of the Word-Men, who believe in textual analysis rather than windy theorising. Maurice Blanchot, whose long study of Lautréamont remains one of the very best critical works, has greatly influenced this group, including many writers associated with the *Tel Quel* magazine, like Marcelin Pleynet and Philippe Sollers, and Lucienne Rochon and Claude Bouché. Alex de Jonge, in *Nightmare Culture* (see pp.147) sums up their approach, with which he largely concurs: "Ducasse is not concerned to tell us what he thinks, but to create a text, an object designed to show us how we all think." Here we are a long way from the stereotype of the suffering poet; from the oversimplifications of such

Lautréamont admirers as Pablo Neruda, who commented in his *Memoirs* that ". . . the promised change in Ducasse's poetry, the swing towards goodness and health, which he did not fulfil, has stirred up much criticism. He is venerated for his sorrow and condemned for his move toward joy"; and from what Nesselroth rightly castigates, "the mistake of a Freudian interpretation such as Marcel Jean and Arpad Mezei's *Maldoror*", which is "that it considers the text as the expression of the experience of an individual, as probably Freud himself would have done, instead of the neurosis of a culture."

Bearing in mind that about ninety authors are mentioned by name in the two slim volumes of the *Poésies* – which are concerned throughout with the function of language and rhetoric – and realising that for Ducasse as for the later Surrealist painters Anna Balakian was discussing in *Surrealism: The Road to the Absolute:* "the important thing was not the choice of object as much as the circumstances of its viewing and its location or position in relation to other things or beings," the stylistic analyses by Nesselroth, Pleynet, Bouché and others, even the erratic Faurisson, have many valuable insights to contribute. Lautréamont-Ducasse's work is subversive, defining and parodying what was no longer required – outworn styles, clichés of thought, literary postures – and this clearing of the decks in the latter half of the nineteenth century has enabled twentieth-century writing to free itself from all restriction. As Octavio Paz recognised: "No one is a poet unless he has felt the temptation to destroy language or create another one, unless he has experienced the fascination of nonmeaning and the no less terrifying fascination of meaning that is inexpressible." Ducasse, on the evidence of the texts, certainly did understand the truth of this statement, and it was also his great achievement to have perceived the narcissism inherent in his own work and in writing in general. Thus the writer, placed at the centre of his images, spun his literary web outwards to include, fascinate, even entrap the reader. He succeeded in constructing a beautiful artefact, delicate yet tough, woven out of the various excretions and endless ramifications of the Self, a semi-transparent maze of meanings that signified all *and* nothing, that would question to deadly effect the conventional linear progression of fiction itself by means of a sort of dazzling cubism that rearranged lines and perspectives, and whose unpredictability had its own wild logic. His work represents a love-hate relationship with the past and with tradition: by means of parody, a key device in his writing, he expresses simultaneously both his nostalgia for that past and his hope for the future.

4.
The Poésies

For so long as there have been men – and men who read Lautréamont – everything has been said and few people have gained anything from it.

(Raoul Vaneigem: *The Revolution of Everyday Life*)

All opinions, Ducasse is saying in the *Poésies*, can be attacked and reversed, just as all words can be rearranged. Nothing is fixed or static. Stasis is death. The idea of a Hall of Fame, a Pantheon of Classics is death. After all, against what did Mervyn's body beat in vain at the end of *Les Chants de Maldoror*? Where *but* the Panthéon itself, the very repository and morgue of fame. Nothing is sacred in the *Poésies*. Ducasse attacks reason and the *Pensées*, thought *and* thoughts, not forgetting the "great" men who leave behind "great" works: unlike Chateaubriand and the others he pillories, Ducasse declares early on that *he* will leave no memoirs! This kind of negation appears a form of literary suicide yet paradoxically it assures him the literary immortality for which he has no use.

We examine a text full of personality and humour to find that "Poetry should be made by all. Not by one." Ducasse referring back to a synthesis of all the senses and methods available? The whole man – all of himself – makes "art", which then becomes the property of all, in all languages, everything anyhow initially acting as grist to the poet's mill. Nothing *should* be privileged in art, and as Paul Zweig notes, this is how Narcissus, no longer isolated, is unmasked and becomes universal.

But this attitude of Ducasse's does not pave the way for community art or pop poetry, nor does it provide a licence for plagiarism as substitute for talent. Plagiarism, like collage, was a device employed to make a point. As when, for example, Ducasse ridicules the "Great-Soft-Heads" by means of absurd lists and epithets, these epithets themselves pithily sum up various aspects of the authors to whom they refer, through a sort of shorthand, just as maxims are a kind of shorthand for philosophy. Where the metamorphoses in *Les Chants de Maldoror* were protean attempts to escape from taboo, morality and laws, in *Poésies* they are linguistic ruses, efforts to break down the tyranny of language itself, ridiculing poetic and philosophic clichés, received ideas and outdated styles, and thereby trying to forge a new kind of language – to be poetic and philosophic at once, both precise and general, both criticism

and creation, for as Octavio Paz writes, "criticism and creation live in permanent symbiosis."

Nothing is new under the sun, and the writer re-works, re-creates old themes, re-interpreting them just as the reader does. The "originality" of the work is therefore beside the point. Vauvenargues himself "corrected" Pascal, approving the principle. Ducasse not only corrects Vauvenargues in *his* turn, but applies the process to himself (or rather to his earlier self — Lautréamont), reworking a passage from *Les Chants de Maldoror*. By changing orders, re-orientating words, different texts emerge, shedding ironic light on their "originals". Gertrude Stein and William Burroughs have *their* predecessors too. ... And Ungaretti over fifty years ago perceptively observed that words in the *Poésies* had been shown to mean everything and nothing. Likenesses can be perceived between anything the author chooses: Ducasse's approach is a *reductio ad absurdum* of Aristotle's views of the poet's function. In *Poésies* truths can be reversed, annihilated by changes of syntax and omission as much as by shifts of context. Classical can be made Romantic or vice versa: terms and labels are meaningless, for we have to learn a new way to read. "Terrorist" to one may signify "freedom fighter" to another, and we all know the real meaning of words like liquidation or phrases like "sensational new offer". Ducasse in one sense leads to the Orwell of *Politics and the English Language* and beyond, to Vaneigem and the Situationists who by shrewd use of collage and juxtaposition exposed both the poverty and richness of slogans, and the thinly veiled hypocrisy of a society which by not respecting words abuses people, and by insulting the intelligence creates a state of political cretinisation in which the various forms of authoritarian control may dominate.

The *Poésies* tell us about both rigidity and flexibility, compression and distortion. In one sense "no matter what its content may be, an aphorism is always true: Pascal, La Rochefoucauld, Vauvenargues can be corrected in the sense of optimism, but the form remains," and yet, Nesselroth (op. cit.) continues, "it was Lautréamont's discovery that the fragmented form of the aphorism is the poetic form which unifies opposites, which is capable of satisfying his *besoin de l'infini*". To adopt a procedure Ducasse might have liked, it is appropriate here to quote Nesselroth quoting Norman O. Brown in turn quoting Bachelard and Blake: "Aphorism is exaggeration or grotesque; in psychoanalysis nothing is true except the exaggerations; and in poetry 'cet extrémisme est le phénomène même de l'élan poétique'. Aphorism is exaggeration, extravagant language; the road of excess which leads to the palace of wisdom. ... Aphorism, the form of the mad truth, the Dionysian form." So much for the view that the *Poésies* are in any way dull or dry. One

remembers Artaud's use of the word "extravagance" in connection with Ducasse, and another comment by that mad re-maker of language: "One point I insist on is that Isidore Ducasse was neither madman nor visionary, but a genius who never ceased for as long as he lived to see with perfect lucidity."

Readers may question whether a "madman" can define or recognise lucidity, but down the centuries the sane have not yet succeeded in defining or recognising madness. It depends which way you look at it, who received what label from whom. This is what Ducasse is trying to tell us. And so this Preface has not been concerned with labelling Ducasse. There has been enough speculation about his personal habits (some of the more ridiculous fabrications by Soupault and Malraux, for example), enough bogus controversy about his supposed drug-addiction, insanity, homosexuality, involvement in radical politics, etc., and guesses at whether his death was through disease such as tuberculosis (see the references to TB in *Les Chants de Maldoror*) or due to smallpox (five hundred Parisian victims in one week in November 1870 – the month Ducasse died). Was it malnutrition? (There are plentiful contemporary accounts of the appalling conditions during the siege.) A drug overdose, assassination, suicide? Does it really matter? Ducasse, cut off by war from both money and relatives, his freedom restricted, fearing perhaps that he would be called up to fight at any moment for an order in which he almost certainly did not believe, hungry like everyone else, but (unlike everyone else) aware of his worldly if not artistic failure, may just have lost the will to live. Outsiders pay a heavy price for existence – material and spiritual – and for Ducasse at twenty-four time, funds and perhaps hope, too, all ran out at once. No memoirs, no grave. Their lack ensures the legend – but let us look instead at the legacy.

The Text

The only known copy of *Poésies* I and II is in the Bibliothèque Nationale, Paris. It was discovered in 1891 by Remy de Gourmont. In 1919 André Breton copied out the full text, which appeared in the magazine *Littérature* (issues 2 and 3), April and May 1919. *Poésies* first appeared in book form, under the imprint *Au Sans Pareil, Paris 1920* with a Preface by Philippe Soupault. The text in this volume is that of the original edition.

The works on Lautréamont mentioned in the Preface are listed either in my Bibliography to *Lautréamont's Maldoror* (London, Allison & Busby, 1970; New York, Thomas Y. Crowell, 1972) or in that included in this book, Volume 2 of the Complete Works. The references throughout to the English translation of *Les Chants de Maldoror* are to the A & B edition, *Lautréamont's Maldoror*.

Acknowledgements

I should like to thank my colleague at Sutton Central Library, Katherine Chedburn, B.A., Dip.Lib., A.I.L., for reading the manuscript of this translation and for her helpful suggestions; also my publishers Clive Allison and Margaret Busby for their enthusiasm over the years for a complete translation of Lautréamont-Ducasse.

A Ducasse Chronology

1846

21 February: Montevideo, Uruguay. Marriage of François Ducasse (b.1809), Deputy Secretary, French Consulate, to Jacquette-Celestine Davezac (b.1821). Bridegroom and bride were both born and bred (at Bazet and Sarniguet respectively) near Tarbes in the Hautes-Pyrenées division of France. Both came from farming families of that region, Ducasse's in particular being large and comparatively prosperous. François Ducasse had been schoolteacher and town clerk at Sarniguet, his new wife's home town, from 1837-9, during which period he probably met her. Some time in 1840 he emigrated to South America and entered the French Consulate as clerk. It has been conjectured that Jacquette Davezac was in service with the Ducasse family at Tarbes; Ducasse was marrying "beneath him". But little is known about her until she joined Ducasse at the altar, seven months pregnant on her wedding day.

4 April: 9 a.m. Birth of their first and only child, probably in the Ducasse house on Calle Camacua.

1847

16 November: This son – very tardily – christened Isidore-Lucien Ducasse at the Metropolitan Church of the Immaculate Conception, Montevideo.

6 December: Death of Isidore's mother, Jacquette Ducasse. No indication on any document of the causes of her early death, nor any trace of her grave. Although Montevideo between 1843 and 1852 was a beleaguered city, under siege by the armies of the bloodthirsty Argentinian dictator Rosas, these *were* mysterious circumstances, especially since Ducasse *père* was a conscientious official working for his government, well aware of formalities to be observed and of decorum. The theory of her suicide, examined by Caradec (op. cit.) and other commentators does not, unlike so much of the inaccuracy and vagueness surrounding Isidore Ducasse's background, seem at all improbable.

1847-59

Little known about the childhood of Isidore Ducasse. His father, François, a well-read, cultured man, reputedly something of a rake, but

highly conscientious in his job, had been promoted to Secretary. Commended by his Consul, and despite a serious attack of yellow fever in 1857, François Ducasse continued to work hard at representing the city's sizeable French community, estimated at between 6,000 and 10,000, and mostly of business people.

1859

July: Isidore Ducasse, aged thirteen, set off on the dangerous two months' sea voyage to France, his destination Tarbes.

October: He entered the Imperial Lycée at Tarbes (now the Lycée Théophile-Gautier), for his age-group two years behind in his work. There he remained until 1862, in all probability spending his school holidays with his uncles and aunts (François Ducasse was the fourth of eight children) in his father's birthplace, Bazet. He was undistinguished at school, his results mediocre except for Latin, Grammar, and Mathematics. Among his friends were Mue and Dazet (q.v.,p.92) who would be dedicatees of the *Poésies*.

1862

August: Left the Lycée and very likely "crammed" with private tutors in order to catch up with studies. No more known until over a year later.

1863

October: Ducasse transferred to the Classics class of the Lycée at Pau (now the Lycée Louis-Barthou), where he was taught by M. Hinstin (q.v.,p.93) another dedicatee to the *Poésies*. His second year was spent in the Philosophy Class, but he never took the two-part *baccalauréat* examination for which these forms prepared.

1865

August: Ducasse left the Lycée, aged nineteen, again with mediocre results – his main successes, such as they were, being in Classics, English, Mathematics and Physics. There are no records of his attending any French universities or the famous Parisian Polytechnic Schools at which Genonceaux (in the Preface to his 1890 edition of *Les Chants de Maldoror*) assumed he would aim. Probability that Ducasse lived at Tarbes for almost the next two years.

1867

21 May: Official records (Hautes-Pyrenées) show that Ducasse was granted a passport to travel to Montevideo.

25 May: Isidore Ducasse embarked from Bordeaux, aboard the *Harrick*. Throughout his entire adolescence, from the ages of thirteen to twenty-one — a third of his whole life in fact — he had not returned home.

End of 1867: Return of Ducasse to France. Lived in Paris hotel, 23 Rue Notre-Dame-des-Victoires, given a generous allowance by his father. François Ducasse had perhaps quarrelled with his son and was glad to be rid of him again after what seems, under the circumstances and considering the long voyage, a very brief homecoming. Possibly as Maurice Saillet (op. cit.) suggests, Isidore might have been in ill health, hence François Ducasse's concern (or guilt-feelings) resulting in an indulgent largesse. Either way, Isidore Ducasse became in effect a sort of remittance man.

1868

August: Chant 1 of *Les Chants de Maldoror* published anonymously, price thirty centimes, by Balitout, Questroy et Cie, 7 Rue Baillif (no longer existing) and 18 Rue de Valois.

15 September: Review by Epistemon in *La Jeunesse* (see p.145).

9 November: Letter I, to an unknown critic (see p.119).

1869

January: Second appearance of Chant 1, this time reprinted at Bordeaux in Evariste Carrance's anthology, *Parfums de l'Ame*, again anonymously.

22 May: Letter II, to the banker Darasse (see p.119). Ducasse needed money to pay Lacroix the remaining 800 francs he owed him for producing the complete *Chants* in book form. The volume was printed and bound that summer.

October: Ducasse moved to 32 Rue du Faubourg-Montmartre. Also in October Poulet-Malassis (see p.146) announced that Ducasse's book could not be published in France.

23 and 27 October: Letters III and IV, to Verboeckhoven (see pp.121 and 123).

1870

January: Brief mention that the book had been published, in Evariste Carrance's new anthology, *Fleurs et Fruits*. Interestingly, Lautréamont was spelt Latréaumont, as was the hero in Eugene Sue's novel of that name (1838).

February: Ducasse moved again, this time to 15 Rue Vivienne (see pp.176-7 of *Lautréamont's Maldoror*, London, 1970).

21 February: Letter V, to Verboeckhoven (see p.125).

12 March: Letter VI, to Darasse (see p.127).

April (between 16-25): First booklet of *Poésies* officially registered with Ministry of Interior.

May: Anonymous review of *Les Chants de Maldoror* appeared in *Bulletin du Bibliophile et Bibliothécaire* (see p.146).

June (between 18-25): Second booklet of *Poésies* registered at Ministry. Both booklets printed by Balitout, Questroy et Cie.

July and August: Two consecutive numbers of the *Revue Populaire de Paris* announced the publication of Ducasse's second booklet. Ducasse was listed as "author of *Maldoror*" and his (new) address given as 7 Faubourg-Montmartre.

19 July: France declared war on Prussia.

September: France was ignominiously defeated by Prussia at Sedan. The Empire fell and the Republic was proclaimed. The siege of Paris began, and with it increasing hardships, a severe winter, chronic food shortages that would lead to famine, a series of epidemics, and constant public unrest.

24 November: Thursday, 8 a.m. Isidore Ducasse died in his hotel at 7 Faubourg-Montmartre. Death certificate (no.2028) signed by hotel proprietor J. F. Dupuis and A. Milleret, one of his staff. Ducasse described on it as *"homme de lettres"* and single. No cause of death given (*sans autres renseignements*).

25 November: The writer buried in temporary grave in the 35th section of the Cimetière du Nord.

1871

20 January: Body exhumed, buried in another temporary resting place in the same cemetery, 49th section. In 1879 this land and surroundings were reclaimed for building purposes by the City of Paris. In such circumstances, remains unclaimed by relatives or friends were usually deposited in the Pantin Ossuary, but as Caradec (op. cit.) has noted there is no record of Ducasse's transfer there nor, indeed, have his researches revealed where any of those buried in section 49 were transferred.

1873

François Ducasse visited Paris (he was soon to retire), probably on business and perhaps also to collect his son's effects and settle the 800 francs debt Isidore had incurred with Lacroix. This visit could explain

why copies of *Les Chants de Maldoror* were put on sale the next year in Brussels, by a French bookshop proprietor there named Jean-Baptiste Rozez. For this edition Rozez changed the cover and an invented printer's name, E. Wittmann, replaced those of Lacroix and Verboeckhoven.

1889

François Ducasse, retired in 1873, died aged eighty in the Hotel des Pyramides, Montevideo, where he had been living since 1875. Ironically, his own death certificate, like his son's, was signed by the hotel owner and one of his employees. Unlike his son however, he left a sizeable fortune – 305,000 francs – and was safely buried in the Central Cemetery, Montevideo.

Meanwhile the "Wittmann" edition of the *Chants* was not successful, but remaindered copies were to find their way back to France at the turn of the century. Many young Belgian writers had already been influenced by the book and discussed it enthusiastically since its original appearance. In 1890 Genonceaux's reprint of *Les Chants de Maldoror* – the book's first true publication in France – set the seal upon Lautréamont's posthumous reputation, which has gone on increasing ever since. Ducasse and the *Poésies*, however, would have to wait still longer for their belated "discovery" – for Remy de Gourmont, Breton and the Surrealists. A delay of thirty more years, before a re-publication that finally opened a literary debate which continues to this day and whose heated controversy would have delighted the author in both his roles – the pseudonymous mystery and the elusive reality.

Poésies

I

*Je remplace la mélancolie par le courage, le doute
par la certitude, le désespoir par l'espoir, la méchanceté
par le bien, les plaintes par le devoir, la scepticisme
par la foi, les sophismes par la froideur
du calme et l'orgueil par la modestie.*

Poésies

I

I replace melancholy with courage, doubt with certainty, despair with hope, wickedness with good, complaints with duty, scepticism with faith, sophisms with the indifference of calm and arrogance with modesty.

A Georges Dazet, Henri Mue, Pedro Zumaran, Louis Durcour, Joseph Bleumstein, Joseph Durand;

A mes condisciples Lespès, Georges Minvielle, Auguste Delmas;

Aux Directeurs de Revues, Alfred Sircos, Frédéric Damé;

Aux Amis passés, présents et futurs;

A Monsieur Hinstin, mon ancien professeur de rhétorique; sont dédiés, une fois pour toutes les autres, les prosaïques morceaux que j'écrirai dans la suite des âges, et dont le premier commence à voir le jour d'hui, typographiquement parlant.

To Georges DAZET, Henri MUE, Pedro ZUMARAN, Louis DURCOUR, Joseph BLEUMSTEIM, Joseph DURAND;
To my fellow-students LESPES, Georges MINVIELLE, Auguste DELMAS;
To the Magazine Editors Alfred SIRCOS, Frédéric DAME;
To FRIENDS past, present and future;
To M. HINSTIN, my former Classics teacher;
are dedicated,[1] once and for all, the prosaic pieces I shall subsequently write, and the first of which here begins to see the light of day, typographically speaking.

Poésies

I

Les gémissements poétiques de ce siècle ne sont que des sophismes.

Les premiers principes doivent être hors de discussion.

J'accepte Euripide et Sophocle; mais je n'accepte pas Eschyle.

Ne faites pas preuve de manque des convenances les plus élémentaires et de mauvais goût envers le créateur.

Repoussez l'incrédulité: vous me ferez plaisir.

Il n'existe pas deux genres de poésies; il n'en est qu'une.

Il existe une convention peu tacite entre l'auteur et le lecteur, par laquelle le premier s'intitule malade, et accepte le second comme garde-malade. C'est le poète qui console l'humanité! Les rôles sont intervertis arbitrairement.

Je ne veux pas être flétri de la qualification de poseur.

Je ne laisserai pas des Mémoires.

La poésie n'est pas la tempête, pas plus que le cyclone. C'est un fleuve majestueux et fertile.

Ce n'est qu'en admettant la nuit physiquement, qu'on est parvenu à la faire passer moralement. O Nuits d'Young! vous m'avez causé beaucoup de migraines!

On ne rêve que lorsque l'on dort. Ce sont des mots comme celui de rêve, néant de la vie, passage terrestre, la préposition peut-être, le trépied désordonné, qui ont infiltré dans vos âmes cette poésie moite des langueurs, pareille à de la pourriture. Passer des mots aux idées, il n'y a qu'un pas.

Les perturbations, les anxiétés, les dépravations, la mort, les exceptions dans l'ordre physique ou moral, l'esprit de négation, les

Poésies

I

The poetic moans of this century are only sophisms.

First principles must be above argument.

I accept Euripides and Sophocles: but I do not accept Aeschylus.[2]

Do not display bad taste and a breach of the most basic proprieties towards the creator.[3]

Repel disbelief: you will give me pleasure.

There are not two kinds of poetry; there is only one.

There exists a far from tacit convention between author and reader, by which the former calls himself patient and accepts the latter as nurse. It is the poet who consoles mankind! The roles are arbitrarily reversed.

I do not want to be branded poseur.

I shall leave no Memoirs.

Poetry is not a tempest, any more than it is a cyclone. It is a majestic and fertile river.

It is only by admitting night physically that one succeeds in doing away with it morally. O *Nights of Young*![4] how many headaches have you caused me!

One dreams only when one is asleep. There are words like those of dream, nothingness of life, earthly thoroughfare, the preposition perhaps, the disordered tripod,[5] which have instilled into your souls this clammy poetry of languor, like that of putrefaction. To pass from words to ideas is but one step.

The disturbances, anxieties, depravities, death, exceptions to the physical or moral order, the spirit of negation, the brutishness,

abrutissements, les hallucinations servies par la volonté, les tourments, la destruction, les renversements, les larmes, les insatiabilités, les asservissements, les imaginations creusantes, les romans, ce qui est inattendu, ce qu'il ne faut pas faire, les singularités chimiques de vautour mystérieux qui guette la charogne de quelque illusion morte, les expériences précoces et avortées, les obscurités à carapace de punaise, la monomanie terrible de l'orgueil, l'inoculation des stupeurs profondes, les oraisons funèbres, les envies, les trahisons, les tyrannies, les impiétés, les irritations, les acrimonies, les incartades agressives, la démence, le splëen, les épouvantements raisonnés, les inquiétudes étranges, que le lecteur préférerait ne pas éprouver, les grimaces, les névroses, les filières sanglantes par lesquelles on fait passer la logique aux abois, les exagérations, l'absence de sincérité, les scies, les platitudes, le sombre, le lugubre, les enfantements pires que les meurtres, les passions, le clan des romanciers de cours d'assises, les tragédies, les odes, les mélodrames, les extrêmes présentés à perpétuité, la raison impunément sifflée, les odeurs de poule mouillée, les affadissements, les grenouilles, les poulpes, les requins, le simoun des déserts, ce qui est somnambule, louche, nocturne, somnifère, noctambule, visqueux, phoque parlant, équivoque, poitrinaire, spasmodique, aphrodisiaque, anémique, borgne, hermaphrodite, bâtard, albinos, pédéraste, phénomène d'aquarium et femme à barbe, les heures soûles du découragement taciturne, les fantaisies, les âcretés, les monstres, les syllogismes démoralisateurs, les ordures, ce qui ne réfléchit pas comme l'enfant, la désolation, ce mancenillier intellectuel, les chancres parfumés, les cuisses aux camélias, la culpabilité d'un écrivain qui roule sur la pente du néant et se méprise lui-même avec des cris joyeux, les remords, les hypocrisies, les perspectives vagues qui vous broient dans leurs engrenages imperceptibles, les crachats sérieux sur les axiômes sacrés, la vermine et ses chatouillements insinuants, les préfaces insensées, comme celles de Cromwell, de Mlle de Maupin et de Dumas fils, les caducités, les impuissances, les blasphèmes, les asphyxies, les étouffements, les rages, — devant ces charniers immondes, que je rougis de nommer, il est temps de réagir enfin contre ce qui nous choque et nous courbe si souverainement.

the hallucinations waited upon by the will, torments, destruction, madnesses, tears, insatiabilities, slaveries, deep-thinking imaginations, novels, the unexpected, things which must not be done, the chemical peculiarities of the mysterious vulture that watches for the carcass of some dead illusion, precocious and abortive experiences, obscurities with a flea-like shell, the terrible obsession with pride, the inoculation with deep stupors, funeral orations, envies, betrayals, tyrannies, impieties, irritations, bitternesses, aggressive tirades, insanity, spleen, rational terrors, strange misgivings the reader would rather not feel, grimaces, neuroses, the cruel routes through which one forces last-ditch logic, exaggerations, lack of sincerity, the nuisances, platitudes, gloom, the dismal, the childbirths worse than murders, passions, the clique of assize-court novelists, tragedies, odes, melodramas, eternally presented extremes, reason hissed off stage with impunity, the odours of wet chicken, dulled tastes, frogs, octopi, sharks, the simoom of the deserts, whatever is clairvoyant, squinting, nocturnal, narcotic, somnambulist, slimy, talking seal, equivocal, consumptive, spasmodic, aphrodisiac, anaemic, one-eyed, hermaphrodite, bastard, albino, pederast, phenomenon of aquarium and bearded lady, the drunken hours of taciturn dejection, the fantasies, pungencies, monsters, demoralising syllogisms, the excrement, whatever is thoughtless as a child, desolation, that intellectual manchineel-tree, perfumed chancres, thighs like camellias, the guilt of a writer who rolls down the slope of nothingness and scorns himself with joyous cries, remorse, hypocrisies, the vague perspectives that grind you within their imperceptible mills, the sober gobs of spittle upon sacred axioms, the insinuating tickling of vermin, idiotic prefaces[6] like those of Cromwell, Mlle de Maupin and Dumas *fils*, the decrepitude, impotence, blasphemies, asphyxiations, fits, rages, – before these foul charnel-houses, which I blush to name, it is time at last to react against what offends us and so imperiously bows us down.

You are being driven incessantly out of your mind and caught in the trap of shadows built with coarse skill by egoism and self-esteem.

Taste is the fundamental quality which sums up all the other

Votre esprit est entraîné perpétuellement hors de ses gonds, et surpris dans le piége de ténèbres construit avec un art grossier par l'égoïsme et l'amour-propre.

Le goût est la qualité fondamentale qui résume toutes les autres qualités. C'est le nec plus ultrà de l'intelligence. Ce n'est que par lui seul que le génie est la santé suprême et l'équilibre de toutes les facultés. Villemain est trente-quatre fois plus intelligent qu' Eugène Sue et Frédéric Soulié. Sa préface du Dictionnaire de l'Académie *verra la mort des romans de Walter Scott, de Fenimore Cooper, de tous les romans possibles et imaginables. Le roman est un genre faux, parce qu'il décrit les passions pour elles-mêmes: la conclusion morale est absente. Décrire les passions n'est rien; il suffit de naître un peu chacal, un peu vautour, un peu panthère. Nous n'y tenons pas. Les décrire, pour les soumettre à une haute moralité, comme Corneille, est autre chose. Celui qui s'abstiendra de faire la première chose, tout en restant capable d'admirer et de comprendre ceux à qui il est donné de faire la deuxième, surpasse, de toute la supériorité des vertus sur les vices, celui qui fait la première.*

Par cela seul qu'un professeur de seconde se dit: "Quand on me donnerait tous les trésors de l'univers, je ne voudrais pas avoir fait des romans pareils à ceux de Balzac et d'Alexandre Dumas," par cela seul, il est plus intelligent qu'Alexandre Dumas et Balzac. Par cela seul qu'un élève de troisième s'est pénétré qu'il ne faut pas chanter les difformités physiques et intellectuelles, par cela seul, il est plus fort, plus capable, plus intelligent que Victor Hugo, s'il n'avait fait que des romans, des drames et des lettres.

Alexandre Dumas fils ne fera jamais, au grand jamais, un discours de distribution des prix pour un lycée. Il ne connaît pas ce que c'est que la morale. Elle ne transige pas. S'il le faisait, il devrait auparavant biffer d'un trait de plume tout ce qu'il a écrit jusqu'ici, en commençant par ses Préfaces absurdes. Réunissez un jury d'hommes compétents: je soutiens qu'un bon élève de seconde est plus fort que lui dans n'importe quoi, même dans la sale question des courtisanes.

Les chefs-d'oeuvre de la langue française sont les discours de

qualities. It is the *nec plus ultra* of the intelligence. Through this alone is genius the supreme health and balance of all the faculties. Villemain[7] is thirty-four times more intelligent than Eugène Sue and Frédéric Soulié.[8] His preface to the *Dictionary of the Academy* will survive Walter Scott's and Fenimore Cooper's novels, and all novels possible and imaginable. The novel is a false genre, since it describes the passions for their own sakes: the moral conclusion is missing. Describing the passions is nothing; it is enough to be born part jackal, part vulture, part panther. We do not hold with that. To describe them in order to submit them to an exalted morality, like Corneille, is another matter. He who refrains from doing the former while remaining capable of admiring and understanding those with the gift of doing the latter, surpasses, with all the superiority of virtue over vice, him who does the former.

For that reason alone a fifth-form teacher who says to himself, "Were they to give me all the treasures of the universe, I should not wish to have written novels like those of Balzac and Alexandre Dumas," for that alone he is more intelligent than Alexandre Dumas and Balzac. For that reason alone when a fourth-form pupil is imbued with the idea that one must not harp on physical and mental deformities, for that alone he is stronger, more capable, more intelligent than Victor Hugo, had he produced only novels, plays and letters.

Alexandre Dumas *fils* will never, never make a school prize-giving speech. He does not know what morality is. It will not compromise. If he were to make one, he would first have to cross out with one stroke of the pen all he has so far written, starting with his absurd Prefaces. Summon a jury of competent men: I maintain that a good fifth-former is superior to him in any respect, even on the *offensive* subject of courtesans.[9]

The masterpieces of the French language are school prize-giving speeches and academic treatises. Indeed, the instruction of youth is perhaps the finest practical expression of duty, and a sound appreciation of Voltaire's works (underline the word appreciation) is preferable to the works themselves. – Of course!

The best authors of novels and plays would in the long run

distribution pour les lycées, et les discours académiques. En effet, l'instruction de la jeunesse est peut-être la plus belle expression pratique du devoir, et une bonne appréciation des ouvrages de Voltaire (creusez le mot appréciation) est préférable à ces ouvrages eux-mêmes. – Naturellement!

Les meilleurs auteurs de romans et de drames dénatureraient à la longue la fameuse idée du bien, si les corps enseignants, conservatoires du juste, ne retenaient les générations jeunes et vieilles dans la voie de l'honnêteté et du travail.

En son nom personnel, malgré elle, il le faut, je viens renier, avec une volonté indomptable, et une ténacité de fer, le passé hideux de l'humanité pleurarde. Oui: je veux proclamer le beau sur une lyre d'or, défalcation faite des tristesses goîtreuses et des fiertés stupides qui décomposent, à sa source, la poésie marécageuse de ce siècle. C'est avec les pieds que je foulerai les stances aigres du scepticisme, qui n'ont pas leur motif d'être. Le jugement, une fois entré dans l'efflorescence de son énergie, impérieux et résolu, sans balancer une seconde dans les incertitudes dérisoires d'une pitié mal placée, comme un procureur général, fatidiquement, les condamne. Il faut veiller sans relâche sur les insomnies purulentes et les cauchemars atrabilaires. Je méprise et j'exècre l'orgueil, et les voluptés infâmes d'une ironie, faite éteignoir, qui déplace la justesse de la pensée.

Quelques caractères, excessivement intelligents, il n'y a pas lieu que vous l'infirmiez par des palinodies d'un goût douteux, se sont jetés, à tête perdue, dans les bras du mal. C'est l'absinthe, savoureuse, je ne le crois pas, mais, nuisible, qui tua moralement l'auteur de Rolla. Malheur à ceux qui sont gourmands! A peine est-il entré dans l'âge mûr, l'aristocrate anglais, que sa harpe se brise sous les murs de Missolonghi, après n'avoir cueilli sur son passage que les fleurs qui couvent l'opium des mornes anéantissements.

Quoique plus grand que les génies ordinaires, s'il s'était trouvé de son temps un autre poète, doué, comme lui, à doses semblables, d'une intelligence exceptionnelle, et capable de se présenter comme son rival, il aurait avoué, le premier, l'inutilité de ses efforts pour produire des malédictions disparates; et que, le bien exclusif est,

distort the well-known idea of the good, if the teaching professions, repositories of what is right, did not keep generations young and old upon the path of honesty and work.

In its personal name, despite it, necessarily, with an indomitable will and an iron tenacity I have come to deny the hideous past of blubbering humanity. Yes: I want to blazon forth the beautiful upon a golden lyre, allowing for the goitrous melancholies and stupid pride that pollute at its source the swampy poetry of this century. I shall trample underfoot the shrill stanzas of scepticism which have no reason for their existence. Judgement, once involved in the efflorescence of its energy, imperious and resolute, without wavering for one second over the ridiculous uncertainties of a misplaced pity, like a public prosecutor, fatefully, condemns them. Without weakening one must guard against purulent insomnias and atrabilious nightmares. I scorn and execrate pride and the infamous delights of an irony employed to extinguish and which displaces precision of thought.

Some characters, excessively intelligent – you have no grounds for invalidating this with recantations in doubtful taste – have hurled themselves head first into the arms of evil. It was absinthe – tasty I rather doubt, but harmful – that morally killed the author[10] of *Rolla*. Woe betide those who are gluttons! Hardly has the English aristocrat reached middle-age before his harp breaks beneath the walls of Missolonghi, having plucked along his way only the blossoms that brew the opium of bleak annihilation.[11]

Although his was an uncommon genius, if during his lifetime there had happened to be another poet like himself endowed with a similar admixture of exceptional intelligence, and capable of coming forward as his rival, he would have been the first to admit the uselessness of his efforts to produce ill-matched maledictions; and that it is good and good alone which, by general consent, is deemed worthy of annexing our esteem. The fact was that there was none effectively to rival him. That is what no one has remarked. How strange! Even on leafing through the anthologies and books of his day we find not one critic who thought to point out the foregoing strict syllogism. And the one to go beyond it need not have invented

seul, déclaré digne, de par la voix de tous les mondes, de s'approprier notre estime. Le fait fut qu'il n'y eut personne pour le combattre avec avantage. Voilà ce qu'aucun n'a dit. Chose étrange! même en feuilletant les recueils et les livres de son époque, aucun critique n'a songé à mettre en relief le rigoureux syllogisme qui précède. Et ce n'est que celui qui la surpassera qui peut l'avoir inventé. Tant on était rempli de stupeur et d'inquiétude, plutôt que d'admiration réfléchie, devant des ouvrages écrits d'une main perfide, mais qui révélaient, cependant, les manifestations imposantes d'une âme qui n'appartient pas au vulgaire des hommes, et qui se trouvait à son aise dans les conséquences dernières d'un des deux moins obscurs problèmes qui intéressent les coeurs non-solitaires: le bien, le mal. Il n'est pas donné à quiconque d'aborder les extrêmes, soit dans un sens, soit dans un autre. C'est ce qui explique pourquoi, tout en louant, sans arrière-pensée, l'intelligence merveilleuse dont il dénote à chaque instant la preuve, lui, un des quatre ou cinq phares de l'humanité, l'on fait, en silence, ses nombreuses réserves sur les applications et l'emploi injustifiables qu'il en a faits sciemment. Il n'aurait pas dû parcourir les domaines sataniques.

La révolte féroce des Troppmann, des Napoléon I, des Papavoine, des Byron, des Victor Noir et des Charlotte Corday sera contenue à distance de mon regard sévère. Ces grands criminels, à des titres si divers, je les écarte d'un geste. Qui croit-on tromper ici, je le demande avec une lenteur qui s'interpose? O dadas de bagne! Bulles de savon! Pantins en baudruche! Ficelles usées! Qu'ils s'approchent, les Konrad, les Manfred, les Lara, les marins qui ressemblent au Corsaire, les Méphistophélès, les Werther, les Don Juan, les Faust, les Iago, les Rodin, les Caligula, les Caïn, les Iridion, les mégères à l'instar de Colomba, les Ahrimane, les manitous manichéens, barbouillés de cervelle, qui cuvent le sang de leurs victimes dans les pagodes sacrées de l'Hindoustan, le serpent, le crapaud et le crocodile, divinités, considérées comme anormales, de l'antique Egypte, les sorciers et les puissances démoniaques du moyen âge, les Prométhée, les Titans de la mythologie foudroyés par Jupiter, les Dieux Méchants vomis par l'imagination primitive des peuples barbares, – toute la série bruyante des diables en carton. Avec la certitude de les

it. One was so filled with astonishment and unease, rather than considered admiration, faced with words written by a treacherous hand, but which nonetheless revealed convincing evidence of a soul that did not belong to the common run of men and found itself at ease with the final outcome of one of the two less obscure problems to interest non-solitary hearts: good, evil. It is not given to anybody to grapple with extremes, whether in one sense or another. Which explains why, while unreservedly praising the marvellous intelligence he manifests at every turn, he, one of the four or five beacons of mankind, one silently makes numerous reservations about the unjustifiable applications and use he has knowingly made of them. He should not have traversed Satanic domains.

The ferocious revolt of the Troppmanns, the Napoleon the Firsts, Papavoines, Byrons, Victor Noirs and Charlotte Cordays shall be contained by my stern gaze.[12] These great criminals with such varied claims, I wave them aside. Whom do they think they are fooling here, I ask myself with an interposing deliberation? O prison-hulk hobby-horses! Soap-bubbles! Gold-leafed puppets! Frayed strings![13] Let them draw near, the Konrads, Manfreds, Laras, the sailors resembling the Corsair, the Mephistopheleses, the Werthers, Don Juans, Fausts, Iagos, Rodins, the Caligulas, Cains, Iridions, the shrews imitating Colomba, the Ahrimans, the Manichean manitous spattered with brains, who ferment their victims' blood in the sacred temples of Hindustan, the serpent, the toad and the crocodile, divinities considered exceptional in ancient Egypt, the sorcerers and demonic forces of the Middle Ages, the Prometheuses, the mythological Titans blasted by Jupiter's thunderbolts, the Evil Gods spewed forth from the primitive imaginations of barbaric races – the whole resounding range of pasteboard devils.[14] Assured of overcoming them, I seize the whip of indignation and of concentration that tries its weight, and await these monsters resolutely, as their predestined tamer.

There are down-at-heel writers, dangerous wags, quadroon jokers, heavy hoaxers, real lunatics, fit to fill Bedlam.[15] Their softening pates, from which screws have worked loose, create gigantic phantoms that sink rather than rise. Scabrous exercise; specious

vaincre, je saisis la cravache de l'indignation et de la concentration qui soupèse, et j'attends ces monstres de pied ferme, comme leur dompteur prévu.

Il y a des écrivains ravalés, dangereux loustics, farceurs au quarteron, sombres mystificateurs, véritables aliénés, qui mériteraient de peupler Bicêtre. Leurs têtes crétinisantes, d'où une tuile a été enlevée, créent des fantômes gigantesques, qui descendent au lieu de monter. Exercice scabreux; gymnastique spécieuse. Passez donc, grotesque muscade. S'il vous plaît, retirez-vous de ma présence, fabricateurs, à la douzaine, de rébus défendus, dans lesquels je n'apercevais pas auparavant, du premier coup, comme aujourd'hui, le joint de la solution frivole. Cas pathologique d'un égoïsme formidable. Automates fantastiques: indiquez-vous du doigt, l'un à l'autre, mes enfants, l'épithète qui les remet à leur place.

S'ils existaient, sous la réalité plastique, quelque part, ils seraient, malgré leur intelligence avérée, mais fourbe, l'opprobre, le fiel, des planètes qu'ils habiteraient la honte. Figurez-vous les, un instant, réunis en société avec des substances qui seraient leurs semblables. C'est une succession non interrompue de combats, dont ne rêveront pas les boule-dogues, interdits en France, les requins et les macrocéphales-cachalots. Ce sont des torrents de sang, dans ces régions chaotiques pleines d'hydres et de minotaures, et d'où la colombe, effarée sans retour, s'enfuit à tire-d'aile. C'est un entassement de bêtes apocalyptiques, qui n'ignorent pas ce qu'elles font. Ce sont des chocs de passions, d'irréconciliabilités et d'ambitions, à travers les hurlements d'un orgueil qui ne se laisse pas lire, se contient, et dont personne ne peut, même approximativement, sonder les écueils et les bas-fonds.

Mais, ils ne m'en imposeront plus. Souffrir est une faiblesse, lorsqu'on peut s'en empêcher et faire quelque chose de mieux. Exhaler les souffrances d'une splendeur non équilibrée, c'est prouver, ô moribonds des maremmes perverses! moins de résistance et de courage, encore. Avec ma voix et ma solennité des grands jours, je te rappelle dans mes foyers déserts, glorieux espoir. Viens t'asseoir à mes côtés, enveloppé du manteau des illusions, sur le trépied raisonnable des apaisements. Comme un meuble de rebut, je t'ai

gymnastics. So hey presto, grotesques. Kindly withdraw from my presence, fabricators of forbidden riddles by the dozen, in which previously I did not spot straight off, as I do today, the trick of the frivolous solution. Pathological case of a fearsome egoism. Fantastic automata: point out to one another, children, the epithet which puts them in their place.

If they existed somewhere in plastic reality they would be, despite their proven but double-dealing intelligence, the opprobrium, the gall, the shame of the planets they inhabited. Picture them for a moment reunited in company with substances that would be their counterparts. It is an uninterrupted succession of combats undreamed of by bulldogs, forbidden in France,[16] by sharks and macrocephalic cachalots. There are torrents of blood in these chaotic regions full of hydras and minotaurs, and whence the dove, frightened off for ever, flies swiftly away. There is a mass of apocalyptic beasts who are not unaware of what they do. These are the collisions of passions, irreconcilabilities and ambitions, through the shrieks of an indecipherable pride that controls itself and whose reefs and depths none, not even approximately, can fathom.

But they shall foist themselves upon me no longer. To suffer is a weakness, when one can prevent it and do something better. To give vent to the sufferings of an unbalanced splendour is to give proof, O moribund ones of the perverse maremmas!, of still less resistance and spirit. With my voice and my broad daylights' solemnity, I call you back to my deserted hearths, glorious hope. Come and sit beside me, wrapped in the cloak of illusions, upon the rational tripod of assurances.[17] Like a piece of cast-off furniture I chased you from my abode with a scorpion-lashed whip. If you wish to convince me that when returning to my home you have forgotten the sorrows which, as tokens of remorse, I once caused you, then damn it, lead back with you that sublime retinue – hold me, I'm fainting! – of offended virtues and their imperishable redresses.

I record bitterly that only a few drops of blood remain in the arteries of our consumptive epochs. Since the odious and odd snivellings, patented without warranty of a trademark, of the Jean-Jacques Rousseaus, the Chateaubriands and wet-nurses in diapers

chassé de ma demeure, avec un fouet aux cordes de scorpions. Si tu souhaites que je sois persuadé que tu as oublié, en revenant chez moi, les chagrins que, sous l'indice des repentirs, je t'ai causés autrefois, crebleu, ramène alors avec toi, cortége sublime, — soutenez-moi, je m'évanouis! — les vertus offensées, et leurs impérissables redressements.

Je constate, avec amertume, qu'il ne reste plus que quelques gouttes de sang dans les artères de nos époques phthisiques. Depuis les pleurnicheries odieuses et spéciales, brevetées sans garantie d'un point de repère, des Jean-Jacques Rousseau, des Châteaubriand et des nourrices en pantalon aux poupons Obermann, à travers les autres poètes qui se sont vautrés dans le limon impur, jusqu'au songe de Jean-Paul, le suicide de Dolorès de Veintemilla, le Corbeau d'Allan, la Comédie Infernale du Polonais, les yeux sanguinaires de Zorilla, et l'immortel cancer, Une Charogne, que peignit autrefois, avec amour, l'amant morbide de la Vénus hottentote, les douleurs invraisemblables que ce siècle s'est créés à lui-même, dans leur voulu monotone et dégoûtant, l'ont rendu poitrinaire. Larves absorbantes dans leurs engourdissements insupportables!

Allez, la musique.

Oui, bonnes gens, c'est moi qui vous ordonne de brûler, sur une pelle, rougie au feu, avec un peu de sucre jaune, le canard du doute, aux lèvres de vermouth, qui répandant, dans une lutte mélancolique entre le bien et le mal, des larmes qui ne viennent pas du cœur, sans machine pneumatique, fait, partout, le vide universel. C'est ce que vous avez de mieux à faire.

Le désespoir, se nourrissant avec un parti pris, de ses fantasmagories, conduit imperturbablement le littérateur à l'abrogation en masse des lois divines et sociales, et à la méchanceté théorique et pratique. En un mot, fait prédominer le derrière humain dans les raisonnements. Allez, et passez-moi le mot! L'on devient méchant, je le répète, et les yeux prennent la teinte des condamnés à mort. Je ne retirerai pas ce que j'avance. Je veux que ma poésie puisse être lue par une jeune fille de quatorze ans.

La vraie douleur est incompatible avec l'espoir. Pour si grande que soit cette douleur, l'espoir, de cent coudées, s'élève plus haut

like Obermann, through to the other poets who have wallowed in the foul slime, right up to the dream of Jean-Paul, Dolores de Veintemilla's suicide, the Raven of Allan, the Pole's Infernal Comedy, the bloodthirsty eyes of Zorilla, and the immortal cancer, A Carcass, once painted lovingly by the morbid lover of the Hottentot Venus, the unlikely sufferings that this century has created for itself have, with their monotonous and disgusting insistence, rendered it consumptive.[18] Absorbent larvae in their unbearable torpors!

Music, ho.

Yes, good people, it is I who direct you to roast upon a red-hot shovel, with a little brown sugar, the duck of doubt with lips of vermouth,[19] which, shedding crocodile tears in a melancholy struggle between good and evil, without an air-pump everywhere brings about the universal vacuum. That is the best thing you can do.

Despair, subsisting with prejudice upon its phantasmagorias, imperturbably leads the man of letters to the wholesale repeal of divine and social laws and to theoretical and practical wickedness. In a word, makes the human arse prevail in arguments. Come on, my turn to speak my piece! One becomes wicked, I repeat, and the eyes take on the hue of men condemned. I shall not retract what I propose. I want my poetry to be fit reading for a fourteen-year-old girl.

True grief is incompatible with hope. Great though this grief may be, hope raises it vastly higher. So leave me alone with the seekers. Down, boy, down, ridiculous bitches, show-offs, *poseurs*! Whatever suffers, whatever dissects the mysteries that surround us, does not hope. Poetry which questions the necessary truths is less fine than that which does not question them. Indecisions to the bitter end, misused talent, time-wasting: nothing easier to prove.

To sing of Adamastor, Jocelyn, Rocambole, is puerile.[20] It is not even as though the author hopes the reader infers that he will pardon his knavish heroes, since he himself betrays them, and relies on the good so as to do without the description of evil. It is in the name of these same virtues Frank[21] misunderstood that we wish to

encore. Donc, laissez-moi tranquille avec les chercheurs. A bas, les pattes, à bas, chiennes cocasses, faiseurs d'embarras, poseurs! Ce qui souffre, ce qui dissèque les mystères qui nous entourent, n'espère pas. La poésie qui discute les vérités nécessaires est moins belle que celle qui ne les discute pas. Indécisions à outrance, talent mal employé, perte de temps: rien ne sera plus facile à vérifier.

Chanter Adamastor, Jocelyn, Rocambole, c'est puéril. Ce n'est même que parce que l'auteur espère que le lecteur sous-entend qu'il pardonnera à ses héros fripons, qu'il se trahit lui-même et s'appuie sur le bien pour faire passer la description du mal. C'est au nom de ces mêmes vertus que Frank a méconnues, que nous voulons bien le supporter, ô saltimbanques des malaises incurables.

Ne faites pas comme ces explorateurs sans pudeur, magnifiques, à leurs yeux, de mélancolie, qui trouvent des choses inconnues dans leur esprit et dans leur corps!

La mélancolie et la tristesse sont déjà le commencement du doute; le doute est le commencement du désespoir; le désespoir est le commencement cruel des différents degrés de la méchanceté. Pour vous en convaincre, lisez la Confession *d'un enfant du siècle. La pente est fatale, une fois qu'on s'y engage. Il est certain qu'on arrive à la méchanceté. Méfiez-vous de la pente. Extirpez le mal par la racine. Ne flattez pas le culte d'adjectifs tels que indescriptible, inénarrable, rutilant, incomparable, colossal, qui mentent sans vergogne aux substantifs qu'ils défigurent: ils sont poursuivis par la lubricité.*

Les intelligences de deuxième ordre, comme Alfred de Musset, peuvent pousser rétivement une ou deux de leurs facultés beaucoup plus loin que les facultés correspondantes des intelligences de premier ordre, Lamartine, Hugo. Nous sommes en présence du déraillement d'une locomotive surmenée. C'est un cauchemar qui tient la plume. Apprenez que l'âme se compose d'une vingtaine de facultés. Parlez-moi de ces mendiants qui ont un chapeau grandiose, avec des haillons sordides!

Voici un moyen de constater l'infériorité de Musset sous les deux poètes. Lisez, devant une jeune fille, Rolla *ou les* Nuits, *les* Fous *de Cobb, sinon les portraits de Gwynplaine et de Dea, ou le*

support him, O mountebanks of incurable malaises.

Do not do as these shameless – in their own eyes, magnificent – explorers of melancholy, who discover things unknown within their minds and bodies!

Melancholy and sadness are the start of doubt, as it is; doubt is the beginning of despair; despair is the cruel beginning of the differing degrees of wickedness. To convince yourself of this, read the *Confession of a child of the century*.[22] The slope downhill is fatal once one is committed to it. It is certain to lead to wickedness. Beware of the slope. Rip out evil by the root. Do not indulge the cult of adjectives such as indescribable, inenarrable, rutilant, incomparable, colossal, which shamelessly lie to the nouns they distort: they are pursued by lewdness.

Second-rate minds, like Alfred de Musset's, can mulishly force one or two of their faculties far further than the corresponding faculties of first-rate minds, Lamartine, Hugo. We are faced with the derailment of an overworked locomotive. It is a nightmare that holds the pen. Learn that the soul is composed of a score of faculties. Talk to me of those beggars who have one grandiose hat, with squalid rags!

Here is a means of establishing Musset's inferiority to the other two poets. Read to a young girl *Rolla* or *The Nights*, *The Fools* by Cobb,[23] or else the portraits of Gwynplaine and Dea,[24] or the speech of Euripides' Theramenes[25] translated into French verse by Racine *père*. She shudders, frowns, raises and lowers her hands aimlessly like a drowning man; her eyes will flash greenish. Read her Victor Hugo's *Prayer for All*. The effects are diametrically opposed. The type of electricity is no longer the same. She bursts out laughing, she asks for more.

Of Hugo nothing will remain but his poems about children, where badness abounds.

Paul and Virginie shocks our deepest aspirations to happiness.[26] In the past, this serial which broods gloomily from the first page to the last, especially the final shipwreck, made me gnash my teeth. I would roll upon the carpet and kick my wooden horse. The description of suffering is a misconception. One should present a

Récit de Théramène d'Euripide, traduit en vers français par Racine le père. Elle tressaille, fronce les sourcils, lève et abaisse les mains, sans but déterminé, comme un homme qui se noie ; les yeux jetteront des lueurs verdâtres. Lisez-lui la Prière pour tous, de Victor Hugo. Les effets sont diamétralement opposés. Le genre d'électricité n'est plus le même. Elle rit aux éclats, elle en demande davantage.

De Hugo, il ne restera que les poésies sur les enfants, où se trouve beaucoup de mauvais.

Paul et Virginie choque nos aspirations les plus profondes au bonheur. Autrefois, cet épisode qui broie du noir de la première à la dernière page, surtout le naufrage final, me faisait grincer des dents. Je me roulais sur le tapis et donnais des coups de pied à mon cheval en bois. La description de la douleur est un contre-sens. Il faut faire voir tout en beau. Si cette histoire était racontée dans une simple biographie, je ne l'attaquerais point. Elle change tout de suite de caractère. Le malheur devient auguste par la volonté impénétrable de Dieu qui le créa. Mais l'homme ne doit pas créer le malheur dans ses livres. C'est ne vouloir, à toutes forces, considérer qu'un seul côté des choses. O hurleurs maniaques que vous êtes!

Ne reniez pas l'immortalité de l'âme, la sagesse de Dieu, la grandeur de la vie, l'ordre qui se manifeste dans l'univers, la beauté corporelle, l'amour de la famille, le mariage, les institutions sociales. Laissez de côté les écrivassiers funestes: Sand, Balzac, Alexandre Dumas, Musset, Du Terrail, Féval, Flaubert, Baudelaire, Leconte et la Grève des Forgerons!

Ne transmettez à ceux qui vous lisent que l'expérience qui se dégage de la douleur, et qui n'est plus la douleur elle-même. Ne pleurez pas en public.

Il faut savoir arracher des beautés littéraires jusque dans le sein de la mort ; mais ces beautés n'appartiendront pas à la mort. La mort n'est ici que la cause occasionnelle. Ce n'est pas le moyen, c'est le but, qui n'est pas elle.

Les vérités immuables et nécessaires, qui font la gloire des nations, et que le doute s'efforce envain d'ébranler, ont commencé depuis les âges. Ce sont des choses auxquelles on ne devrait pas

rosy view of things. If that story were related in an ordinary biography, I would not be attacking it at all. It changes character at once. Misfortune becomes august through the impenetrable will of God who created it. But man must not create misfortune in his books. This is to want, despite all opposition, to consider only one side of things. O maniacal ravers that you are!

Do not deny the immortality of the soul, the wisdom of God, the grandeur of life, the order manifest in the universe, physical beauty, love of family, marriage, the social institutions. Discard the dismal hacks:[27] Sand, Balzac, Alexandre Dumas, Musset, Du Terrail, Féval, Flaubert, Baudelaire, Leconte and the *Blacksmiths' Strike*!

Convey to your readers only the experience which emerges from suffering and which is no longer the suffering itself. Do not weep in public.

One must know how to snatch literary beauty from the very bosom of death; but these beauties do not belong to death. Death is here only the occasional cause. It is not the means, it is the end – which it is not.

The immutable and necessary truths which are the glory of nations, and which doubt strives in vain to shake, began ages ago. These are things one should not touch. Those who would make literary anarchy under the pretext of novelty lapse into error. One does not dare attack God; one attacks the immortality of the soul. Yet the immortality of the soul, that too, is as old as the world's foundations. What other belief will replace it, if replaced it must be? It will not always be a negation.

If one recalls the truth whence all the others flow, God's absolute goodness and his absolute ignorance of evil, sophisms will collapse of their own accord. At the very same time there shall collapse the rather unpoetic literature which relied upon them. All literature which debates the eternal axioms is condemned to live only off itself. It is unjust. It devours its liver. The *novissima Verba*[28] make the snotty third-formers smile haughtily. We do not have the right to question the Creator on anything whatsoever.

toucher. *Ceux qui veulent faire de l'anarchie en littérature, sous prétext de nouveau, tombent dans le contre-sens. On n'ose pas attaquer Dieu; on attaque l'immortalité de l'âme. Mais, l'immortalité de l'âme, elle aussi, est vieille comme les assises du monde. Quelle autre croyance la remplacera, si elle doit être remplacée? Ce ne sera pas toujours une négation.*

Si l'on se rappelle la vérité d'où découlent toutes les autres, la bonté absolue de Dieu et son ignorance absolue du mal, les sophismes s'effondreront d'eux-mêmes. S'effondrera, dans un temps pareil, la littérature peu poétique qui s'est appuyée sur eux. Toute littérature qui discute les axiômes éternels est condamnée à ne vivre que d'elle-même. Elle est injuste. Elle se dévore le foie. Les novissima Verba *font sourire superbement les gosses sans mouchoir de la quatrième. Nous n'avons pas le droit d'interroger le Créateur sur quoi que ce soit.*

Si vous êtes malheureux, il ne faut pas le dire au lecteur. Gardez cela pour vous.

Si on corrigeait les sophismes dans le sens des vérités correspondantes à ces sophismes, ce n'est que la correction qui serait vraie; tandis que la pièce ainsi remaniée, aurait le droit de ne plus s'intituler fausse. Le reste serait hors du vrai, avec trace de faux, par conséquent nul, et considéré, forcément, comme non avenu.

La poésie personnelle a fait son temps de jongleries relatives et de contorsions contingentes. Reprenons le fil indestructible de la poésie impersonnelle, brusquement interrompu depuis la naissance du philosophe manqué de Ferney, depuis l'avortement du grand Voltaire.

Il paraît beau, sublime, sous prétexte d'humilité ou d'orgueil, de discuter les causes finales, d'en fausser les conséquences stables et connues. Détrompez-vous, parce qu'il n'y a rien de plus bête! Renouons la chaîne régulière avec les temps passés; la poésie est la géométrie par excellence. Depuis Racine, la poésie n'a pas progressé d'un millimètre. Elle a reculé. Grâce à qui? aux Grandes-Têtes-Molles de notre époque. Grâce aux femmelettes, Châteaubriand, le Mohican-Mélancolique; Sénancourt, l'Homme-en-Jupon; Jean-Jacques Rousseau, le Socialiste-Grincheur; Anne Radcliffe, le

If you are unhappy, you must not tell the reader so. Keep it to yourself.

If one were to correct sophisms via the truths associated with these sophisms, the correction alone would be true; while the work thus recast would have the right not to call itself false any more. The rest would be out of true, with a trace of falsehood, and therefore of necessity considered null and void.

Personal poetry has had its day of relative juggling tricks and contingent contortions. Let us take up the indestructible thread of impersonal poetry, abruptly cut short since the birth of the would-be philosopher of Ferney,[29] since the miscarriage of the great Voltaire.

It seems fine, sublime, under the pretext of humility or pride, to argue about final causes, to falsify their stable and known consequences. Disabuse yourselves, for there is nothing more foolish! Let us again link together the orderly chain with bygone times; poetry is geometry in the highest sense. Since Racine, poetry has not progressed one millimetre. It has regressed. Thanks to whom? Thanks to the Great-Soft-Heads of our epoch. Thanks to the old ninnies, Châteaubriand, the Melancholy-Mohican; Sénancourt, the Man-in-a-Petticoat; Jean-Jacques Rousseau, the Socialist-Grouser; Anne Radcliffe, the Crazy-Spectre; Edgar Poë, the Mameluke-of-Alcohol-Dreams; Mathurin, the Accomplice-of-Darkness; Georges Sand, the Circumcised-Hermaphrodite; Théophile Gautier, the Incomparable-Grocer; Leconte, the Devil's-Captive; Goethe, the Suicide-through-Weeping; Sainte-Beuve, the Suicide-through-Laughter; Lamartine, the Maudlin-Stork; Lermontoff, the Tiger-who-Howls; Victor Hugo, the Funereal-Green-Spindleshanks; Misçkiéwicz, the Imitator-of-Satan; Musset, the Shirtless-Intellectual - Dandy; and Byron, the Hippopotamus - of - the - Infernal - Jungles.[30]

Doubt has existed at all times in the minority. In this century it is in the majority. We breathe the violation of duty through the pores. That is only evident once; it will never be seen again.

The notions of plain reason have been so obscured nowadays that the first thing third-form teachers do when instructing their

Spectre-Toqué; Edgar Poë, le Mameluck-des-Rêves-d'Alcool; Mathurin, le Compère-des-Ténèbres; Georges Sand, l'Hermaphrodite-Circoncis; Théophile Gautier, l'Incomparable-Epicier; Leconte, le Captif-du-Diable; Goethe, le Suicidé-pour-Pleurer; Saint-Beuve, le Suicidé-pour-Rire; Lamartine, la Cigogne-Larmoyante; Lermontoff, le Tigre-qui-Rugit; Victor Hugo, le Funèbre-Echalas-Vert; Misçkiéwicz, l'Imitateur-de-Satan; Musset, le Gandin-Sans-Chemise-Intellectuelle; et Byron, l'Hippopotame-des-Jungles-Infernales.

Le doute a existé de tout temps en minorité. Dans ce siècle, il est en majorité. Nous respirons la violation du devoir par les pores. Cela ne s'est vu qu'une fois; cela ne se reverra plus.

Les notions de la simple raison sont tellement obscurcies à l'heure qu'il est, que, la première chose que font les professeurs de quatrième, quand ils apprennent à faire des vers latins à leurs élèves, jeunes poètes dont la lèvre est humectée du lait maternel, c'est de leur dévoiler par la pratique le nom d'Alfred de Musset. Je vous demande un peu, beaucoup! Les professeurs de troisième, donc, donnent, dans leurs classes à traduire, en vers grecs, deux sanglants épisodes. Le premier, c'est la repoussante comparaison du pélican. Le deuxième, sera l'épouvantable catastrophe arrivée à un laboureur. A quoi bon regarder le mal? N'est-il pas en minorité? Pourquoi pencher la tête d'un lycéen sur des questions qui, faute de n'avoir pas été comprises, ont fait perdre la leur à des hommes tels que Pascal et Byron?

Un élève m'a raconté que son professeur de seconde avait donné à sa classe, jour par jour, ces deux charognes à traduire en vers hébreux. Ces plaies de la nature animale et humaine le rendirent malade pendant un mois, qu'il passa à l'infirmerie. Comme nous nous connaissions, il me fit demander par sa mère. Il me raconta, quoique avec naïveté, que ses nuits étaient troublées par des rêves de persistance. Il croyait voir une armée de pélicans qui s'abattaient sur sa poitrine, et la lui déchiraient. Ils s'envolaient ensuite vers une chaumière en flammes. Ils mangeaient la femme du laboureur et ses enfants. Le corps noirci de brûlures, le laboureur sortait de la maison, engageait avec les pélicans un combat atroce. Le tout se précipitait dans la chaumière, qui retombait en éboulements. De la

pupils, young poets whose lips are still moist with their mothers' milk, how to write Latin verse, is reveal to them through practice the name of Alfred de Musset. Well, I ask you! So fourth-form teachers in their classes set two bloody episodes for translation into Greek verse. The first is the repulsive simile of the pelican. The second being the dreadful catastrophe that befell a labourer. What is the use of contemplating evil? Is it not in the minority? Why weigh down a schoolchild's head with questions which, for want of being understood, caused men like Pascal[31] and Byron to lose theirs?

A pupil told me that his fifth-form teacher had given his class, day after day, these two cadavers to translate into Hebrew verse.[32] These plagues of animal and human nature made him ill for a month, which he spent in the infirmary. As we know each other, he got his mother to call for me. He told me, somewhat naively, that his nights were troubled by recurrent dreams. He thought he saw an army of pelicans that swooped upon his chest and ripped it out of him. Then they flew off towards a thatched cottage in flames. They were devouring the labourer's wife and children. His body charred by burns, the labourer would come out of the house and engage in a frightful struggle with the pelicans. They would all rush headlong into the cottage, which would collapse in ruins. From the heaped mass of rubble – this never failed – he would see his fifth-form teacher emerge, holding in one hand his heart, in the other a sheet of paper on which could be deciphered, in lines of brimstone, the passages about the pelican and the labourer, just as Musset himself composed them. It was not easy at first sight to diagnose his type of illness. I enjoined him to be sure to stay silent and to talk about it to no one, especially not to his fifth-form teacher. I advised his mother to keep him at home with her for a few days, assuring her that this would pass. Indeed, I took pains to visit him for a few hours each day, and it passed off.

Criticism must attack the form, never the content of your ideas, of your language. Settle it among yourselves.

The feelings are the most incomplete form of reasoning that can be imagined.

All the water in the sea would not suffice to wash away one intellectual bloodstain.[33]

masse soulevée des décombres – cela ne ratait jamais – il voyait sortir son professeur de seconde, tenant d'une main son cœur, de l'autre une feuille de papier où l'on déchiffrait, en traits de soufre, la comparaison du pélican et celle du laboureur, telles que Musset lui-même les a composées. Il ne fut pas facile, au premier abord, de pronostiquer son genre de maladie. Je lui recommandai de se taire soigneusement, et de n'en parler à personne, surtout à son professeur de seconde. Je conseillai à sa mère de le prendre quelques jours chez elle, en assurant que cela se passerait. En effet, j'avais soin d'arriver chaque jour pendant quelques heures, et cela se passa.

Il faut que la critique attaque la forme, jamais le fond de vos idées, de vos phrases. Arrangez-vous.

Les sentiments sont la forme de raisonnement la plus incomplète qui se puisse imaginer.

Tout l'eau de la mer ne suffirait pas à laver une tache de sang intellectuelle.

Poésies

II

II

Le génie garantit les facultés du cœur.

L'homme n'est pas moins immortel que l'âme.

Les grandes pensées viennent de la raison!

La fraternité n'est pas un mythe.

Les enfants qui naissent ne connaissent rien de la vie, pas même la grandeur.

Dans le malheur, les amis augmentent.

Vous qui entrez, laissez tout désespoir.

Bonté, ton nom est homme.

C'est ici que demeure la sagesse des nations.

Chaque fois que j'ai lu Shakespeare, il m'a semblé que je déchiquète le cervelle d'un jaguar.

J'écrirai mes pensées avec ordre, par un dessein sans confusion. Si elles sont justes, la première venue sera la conséquence des autres. C'est le véritable ordre. Il marque mon objet par le désordre calligraphique. Je ferais trop de déshonneur à mon sujet, si je ne le traitais pas avec ordre. Je veux montrer qu'il en est capable.

Je n'accepte pas le mal. L'homme est parfait. L'âme ne tombe pas. Le progrès existe. Le bien est irréductible. Les antéchrists, les anges accusateurs, les peines éternelles, les religions sont le produit du doute.

Dante, Milton, décrivant hypothétiquement les landes infernales, ont prouvé que c'étaient des hyènes de première espèce. La preuve est excellente. Le résultat est mauvais. Leurs ouvrages ne s'achètent pas.

L'homme est un chêne. La nature n'en compte pas de plus robuste. Il ne faut pas que l'univers s'arme pour le défendre. Une goutte d'eau ne suffit pas à sa préservation. Même quand l'univers le défendrait, il ne serait pas plus déshonoré que ce qui ne le préserve pas. L'homme sait que son règne n'a pas de mort, que l'univers possède un commencement. L'univers ne sait rien: c'est, tout au plus, un roseau pensant.

II

Genius guarantees the faculties of the heart.[34]
Man is no less immortal than the soul.
Great thoughts spring from reason![35]
Fraternity is not a myth.
Newborn children know nothing of life, not even its greatness.
In misfortune, friends increase.[36]
Abandon all despair, ye who enter here.[37]
Goodness, thy name is man.[38]
Herein resides the wisdom of nations.

Each time I read Shakespeare it seems to me that I cut to shreds the brain of a jaguar.

I shall write down my thoughts in order, to a plan without confusion. If they are correct, the first will be the consequence of the others. It is the true order. It characterises my object by calligraphic disorder. I should disgrace my subject too much were I not to treat it with order. I want to show that it is capable of this.[39]

I do not accept evil. Man is perfect. The soul does not topple. Progress exists. Good is irreducible. Antichrists, accusing angels, eternal sufferings, religions, are the products of doubt.

Dante, Milton, hypothetically describing the infernal wastelands, have proved themselves first-class hyenas. The proof is excellent. The result bad. Their works are not bought.

Man is an oak. Nature contains nothing sturdier. The universe need not arm itself to defend him. A drop of water is not enough to preserve him. Even if the universe were to defend him, he would no more be dishonoured than whatever does not protect him. Man knows that his reign has no death, that the universe boasts a beginning. The universe knows nothing: it is at best a thinking reed.[40]

I imagine Elohim to be cold rather than sentimental.[41]

Love of a woman is incompatible with love of humanity. Imperfection must be rejected. Nothing is more imperfect than shared[42] egoism. Throughout life, suspicions, recriminations, solemn oaths

Je me figure Elohim plutôt froid que sentimental.

L'amour d'une femme est incompatible avec l'amour de l'humanité. L'imperfection doit être rejetée. Rien n'est plus imparfait que l'égoïsme à deux. Pendant la vie, les défiances, les récriminations, les serments écrits dans la poudre pullulent. Ce n'est plus l'amant de Chimène; c'est l'amant de Graziella. Ce n'est plus Pétrarque; c'est Alfred de Musset. Pendant la mort, un quartier de roche auprès de la mer, un lac quelconque, la forêt de Fontainebleau, l'île d'Ischia, un cabinet de travail en compagnie d'un corbeau, une chambre ardente avec un crucifix, un cimetière où surgit, aux rayons d'une lune qui finit par agacer, l'objet aimé, des stances où un groupe de filles dont on ne sait pas le nom, viennent balader à tour de rôle, donner la mesure de l'auteur, font entendre des regrets. Dans les deux cas, la dignité ne se retrouve point.

L'erreur est la légende douloureuse.

Les hymnes à Elohim habituent la vanité à ne pas s'occuper des choses de la terre. Tel est l'écueil des hymnes. Ils déshabituent l'humanité à compter sur l'écrivain. Elle le délaisse. Elle l'appelle mystique, aigle, parjure à sa mission. Vous n'êtes pas la colombe cherchée.

Un pion pourrait se faire un bagage littéraire, en disant le contraire de ce qu'ont dit les poètes de ce siècle. Il remplacerait leurs affirmations par des négations. Réciproquement. S'il est ridicule d'attaquer les premiers principes, il est plus ridicule de les défendre contre ces mêmes attaques. Je ne les défendrai pas.

Le sommeil est une récompense pour les uns, un supplice pour les autres. Pour tous, il est une sanction.

Si la morale de Cléopâtre eût été moins courte, la face de la terre aurait changé. Son nez n'en serait pas devenu plus long.

Les actions cachées sont les plus estimables. Lorsque j'en vois tant dans l'histoire, elles me plaisent beaucoup. Elles n'ont pas été tout à fait cachées. Elles ont été sues. Ce peu, par où elles ont paru, en augmente le mérite. C'est le plus beau de n'avoir pas pu les cacher.

Le charme de la mort n'existe que pour les courageux.

L'homme est si grand, que sa grandeur paraît surtout en ce

written in dust, pullulate. It is no longer the lover of Chimene; it is the lover of Graziella. It is no longer Petrarch; it is Alfred de Musset.⁴³ While dying, a rocky area close by the sea, any old lake, the forest of Fontainebleau, the island of Ischia, a study complete with raven, a chambre ardente with a crucifix,⁴⁴ a cemetery where the object of one's love looms in view amid moonbeams that finally annoy, stanzas wherein a group of unnamed maidens come and stroll in turn, showing off the author's ability, uttering regrets. In both cases, seriousness doesn't enter into it at all.⁴⁵

The mistake is the mournful tale.

Hymns to Elohim accustom vanity not to be concerned with earthly things. Such is the snag of hymns. They wean mankind from relying upon the writer. It forsakes him. It calls him mystic, eagle, perjurer of his mission. You are not the sought-after dove.⁴⁶

An assistant schoolmaster could manufacture a literary outfit for himself by stating the contrary of what the poets of this century have said. He would replace their affirmations with negations. And vice versa. If it is ridiculous to attack first principles, it is more ridiculous to defend them against these same attacks. I shall not defend them.⁴⁷

Sleep is a reward for some, a punishment for others. For all, it is a sanction.

If Cleopatra's morals had been less short, the face of the world would have changed. Her nose would have grown no longer.⁴⁸

Concealed actions are the most estimable. When I see a few of these in history, they please me greatly. They have not been completely concealed. They have been known. This small way in which they appeared increases their merit. That they could not be concealed is the finest thing of all.⁴⁹

The charm of death exists only for the brave.

Man is so great that his greatness is especially apparent in that he does not want to acknowledge his unhappiness. A tree does not know it is great. To be great is to know one is great. To be great is not to want to acknowledge one's unhappiness. His greatness refutes these miseries. Greatness of a king.⁵⁰

When I write down my thoughts, they do not escape me. This

qu'il ne veut pas se connaître misérable. Un arbre ne se connaît pas grand. C'est être grand que de se connaître grand. C'est être grand que de ne pas vouloir se connaître misérable. Sa grandeur réfute ces misères. Grandeur d'un roi.

Lorsque j'écris ma pensée, elle ne m'échappe pas. Cette action me fait souvenir de ma force que j'oublie à toute heure. Je m'instruis à proportion de ma pensée enchaînée. Je ne tends qu'à connaître la contradiction de mon esprit avec le néant.

Le cœur de l'homme est un livre que j'ai appris à estimer.

Non imparfait, non déchu, l'homme n'est plus le grand mystère.

Je ne permets à personne, pas même à Elohim, de douter de ma sincérité.

Nous sommes libres de faire le bien.

Le jugement est infaillible.

Nous ne sommes pas libres de faire le mal.

L'homme est le vainqueur des chimères, la nouveauté de demain, la régularité dont gémit le chaos, le sujet de la conciliation. Il juge de toutes choses. Il n'est pas imbécile. Il n'est pas ver de terre. C'est le dépositaire du vrai, l'amas de certitude, la gloire, non le rebut de l'univers. S'il s'abaisse, je le vante. S'il se vante, je le vante davantage. Je le concilie. Il parvient à comprendre qu'il est la sœur de l'ange.

Il n'y a rien d'incompréhensible.

La pensée n'est pas moins claire que le cristal. Une religion, dont les mensonges s'appuient sur elle, peut la troubler quelques minutes, pour parler de ces effets qui durent longtemps. Pour parler de ces effets qui durent peu de temps, un assassinat de huit personnes aux portes d'une capitale, la troublera – c'est certain – jusqu'à la destruction du mal. La pensée ne tarde pas à reprendre sa limpidité.

La poésie doit avoir pour but la vérité pratique. Elle énonce les rapports qui existent entre les premiers principes et les vérités secondaires de la vie. Chaque chose reste à sa place. La mission de la poésie est difficile. Elle ne se mêle pas aux événements de la politique, à la manière dont on gouverne un peuple, ne fait pas

action makes me remember my strength which I forget at all times. I educate myself proportionately to my captured[51] thought. I aim only to distinguish the contradiction between my mind and nothingness.[52]

Man's heart is a book I have learned to value.

Not imperfect, not fallen, man is no longer the great mystery.

I allow no one, not even Elohim, to doubt my sincerity.

We are free to do good.

Judgement is infallible.

We are not free to do evil.

Man is the conqueror of chimeras, the novelty of tomorrow, the regularity which chaos bemoans, the subject of conciliation. He is the judge of all things. He is not a half-wit. He is no worm. He is truth's trustee, the store of certainty, the glory, not the outcast of the universe. If he humbles himself, I extol him. If he extols himself, I extol him the more. I reconcile him. He comes to understand that he is the angel's sister.[53]

Nothing is incomprehensible.

Thought is quite as clear as crystal. A religion whose lies depend upon it may cloud it momentarily, speaking of long-term effects. Speaking of short-term effects, an assassination of eight persons at the gates of a capital will cloud it – that's for certain – until the destruction of evil.[54] Thought is not slow to regain clarity.

Poetry must have as its aim practical truth. It states the connections that exist between the first principles and the secondary truths of life. Each thing stays where it is. The mission of poetry is difficult. It does not dabble in political events, in the way a nation is governed, nor allude to periods of history, coups d'état, regicides, court intrigues. It does not tell of battles man fights, by way of exception, with himself and his passions. It discovers the laws that keep political theory going, universal peace, the refutations of Machiavelli,[55] the wrapping paper of which Proudhon's works consist,[56] the psychology of mankind. A poet must be more useful than any other member of his tribe. His work is the code of diplomats, legislators, teachers of youth. We are a long way from the Homers, Virgils, Klopstocks, Camoënses,[57] from imaginations run wild, ode-

allusion aux périodes historiques, aux coups d'Etat, aux régicides, aux intrigues des cours. Elle ne parle pas des luttes que l'homme engage, par exception, avec lui-même, avec ses passions. Elle découvre les lois qui font vivre la politique théorique, la paix universelle, les réfutations de Machiavel, les cornets dont se composent les ouvrages de Proudhon, la psychologie de l'humanité. Un poète doit être plus utile qu'aucun citoyen de sa tribu. Son œuvre est le code des diplomates, des législateurs, des instructeurs de la jeunesse. Nous sommes loin des Homère, des Virgile, des Klopstock, des Camoëns, des imaginations émancipées, des fabricateurs d'odes, des marchands d'épigrammes contre la divinité. Revenons à Confucius, au Boudha, à Socrate, à Jésus-Christ, moralistes qui couraient les villages en souffrant de faim! Il faut compter désormais avec la raison, qui n'opère que sur les facultés qui président à la catégorie des phénomènes de la bonté pure.

Rien n'est plus naturel que de lire le Discours de la Méthode *après avoir lu* Bérénice. *Rien n'est moins naturel que de lire le* Traité de l'Induction *de Biéchy, le* Problème du Mal *de Naville, après avoir lu les* Feuilles d'Automne, *les* Contemplations. *La transition se perd. L'esprit regimbe contre la ferraille, la mystagogie. Le cœur est ahuri devant ces pages qu'un fantoche griffonna. Cette violence l'éclaire. Il ferme le livre. Il verse une larme à la mémoire des auteurs sauvages. Les poètes contemporains ont abusé de leur intelligence. Les philosophes n'ont pas abusé de la leur. Le souvenir des premiers s'éteindra. Les derniers sont classiques.*

Racine, Corneille, auraient été capables de composer les ouvrages de Descartes, de Malebranche, de Bâcon. L'âme des premiers est une avec celle des derniers. Lamartine, Hugo, n'auraient pas été capables de composer le Traité de l'Intelligence. *L'âme de son auteur n'est pas adéquate avec celle des premiers. La fatuité leur a fait perdre les qualités centrales. Lamartine, Hugo, quoique supérieurs à Taine, ne possèdent, comme lui, que des – il est pénible de faire cet aveu – facultés secondaires.*

Les tragédies excitent la pitié, la terreur, par le devoir. C'est quelque chose. C'est mauvais. Ce n'est pas si mauvais que le lyrisme moderne. La Médée *de Legouvé est préférable à la collection des*

manufacturers, vendors of epigrams against the divinity. Let us return to Confucius, Buddha, Socrates, Jesus Christ, moralists who roamed the villages while suffering from hunger! From now on one must reckon with reason, which only operates upon the faculties presiding over the category of phenomena of pure goodness.

Nothing is more natural than to read the *Discourse on Method* after reading *Bérénice*.[58] Nothing is less natural than to read Biéchy's *Treatise on Induction* and Naville's *Problem of Evil*,[59] after reading *Autumn Leaves* and *Contemplations*.[60] The transition is lost. The mind baulks at the junk, the mystagogy. The heart is bewildered by these pages scrawled by a marionnette. This violence enlightens him. He shuts the book. He sheds a tear in remembrance of the unsociable[61] authors. Contemporary poets have abused their intelligence. The philosophers have not abused theirs. Memory of the former will fade. The latter are classics.

Racine, Corneille, would have been capable of writing the works of Descartes, Malebranche,[62] and Bacon. The souls of the former are at one with those of the latter. Lamartine, Hugo, would have been incapable of composing the *Treatise on the Intelligence*.[63] The soul of its author is not on a par with those of the former. Self-satisfaction made them lose their central qualities. Lamartine, Hugo, though Taine's superiors, like him possess only – it is painful to admit this – minor talents.

Tragedies arouse pity and terror through duty. That is something. It is bad. But not as bad as modern lyricism. Legouve's *Medea* is preferable to the collective works of Byron, Capendu, Zaccone, Félix, Gagne, Gaboriau, Lacordaire, Sardou, Goethe, Ravignan, Charles Diguet.[64] Which writer among you, pray, can lift – what is it? What are these snorts from the opposition? – the weight of *Augustus's Monologue*![65] Hugo's barbarous vaudevilles do not proclaim duty. The melodramas of Racine and Corneille, the novels of La Calprenède, do.[66] Lamartine is not capable of writing Pradon's *Phèdre;* Hugo of Rotrou's *Wenceslas;* Sainte-Beuve, the tragedies of Laharpe and Marmontel.[67] Musset is capable of coining proverbs. Tragedy is an involuntary error, allows struggle, is good's first step, will not appear in this work. It retains its prestige. The same does

ouvrages de Byron, de Capendu, de Zaccone, de Félix, de Gagne, de Gaboriau, de Lacordaire, de Sardou, de Gœthe, de Ravignan, de Charles Diguet. Quel écrivain d'entre vous, je prie, peut soulever — qu'est-ce? Quels sont ces reniflements de la résistance? — Le poids du Monologue d'Auguste! Les vaudevilles barbares de Hugo ne proclament pas le devoir. Les mélodrames de Racine, de Corneille, les romans de la Calprenède le proclament. Lamartine n'est pas capable de composer la Phèdre de Pradon; Hugo, le Venceslas de Rotrou; Sainte-Beuve, les tragédies de Laharpe, de Marmontel. Musset est capable de faire des proverbes. La tragédie est une erreur involontaire, admet la lutte, est le premier pas du bien, ne paraîtra pas dans cet ouvrage. Elle conserve son prestige. Il n'en est pas de même du sophisme, — après — coup le gongorisme métaphysique des auto-parodistes de mon temps héroïco-burlesque.

Le principe des cultes est l'orgueil. Il est ridicule d'adresser la parole à Elohim, comme ont fait les Job, les Jérémie, les David, les Salomon, les Turquéty. La prière est un acte faux. La meilleure manière de lui plaire est indirecte, plus conforme à notre force. Elle consiste à rendre notre race heureuse. Il n'y a pas deux manières de plaire à Elohim. L'idée du bien est une. Ce qui est le bien en moins l'étant en plus, je permets que l'on me cite l'exemple de la maternité. Pour plaire à sa mère, un fils ne lui criera pas qu'elle est sage, radieuse, qu'il se conduira de façon à mériter la plupart de ses éloges. Il fait autrement. Au lieu de le dire lui-même, il le fait penser par ses actes, se dépouille de cette tristesse qui gonfle les chiens de Terre-Neuve. Il ne faut pas confondre la bonté d'Elohim avec la trivialité. Chacun est vraisemblable. La familiarité engendre le mépris; la vénération engendre le contraire. Le travail détruit l'abus des sentiments.

Nul raisonneur ne croit contre sa raison.

La foi est une vertu naturelle par laquelle nous acceptons les vérités qu'Elohim nous révèle par la conscience.

Je ne connais pas d'autre grâce que celle d'être né. Un esprit impartial la trouve complète.

La bien est la victoire sur le mal, la négation du mal. Si l'on chante le bien, le mal est éliminé par cet acte congru. Je ne chante

not hold true of the sophism – metaphysical Gongorism after the event – of the self-parodists of my mock-heroic times.⁶⁸

The principle of worship is pride. It is ridiculous to address Elohim as did Job, Jeremiah, David, Solomon, Turquéty.⁶⁹ Prayer is a false act. The best way to please him is indirect, more in keeping with our strength. It consists in making our race happy. There are no two ways of pleasing Elohim. The concept of the good is indivisible. Since virtue in little is virtue in much, I allow mention of the example of maternity. To please his mother, a son will not proclaim to her that she is modest, radiant, that he will behave himself so as to merit most of her praises. He does otherwise. Instead of saying it himself, he reminds her by his actions, rids himself of that sadness that puffs up Newfoundland dogs. One must not confuse Elohim's goodness with triviality. Each is to be presumed. Familiarity breeds contempt; veneration breeds the opposite. Work destroys misuse of the feelings.

No reasoner believes contrary to his reason.

Faith is a natural virtue by which we accept the truths Elohim reveals to us through conscience.

I am aware of no blessing other than that of being born. An impartial spirit finds it complete.

Good is victory over evil, the negation of evil. If one sings of good, evil is eliminated by this congruous act. I do not sing of what must not be done. I sing of what needs to be done. The former does not contain the latter. The latter contains the former.⁷⁰

Youth listens to the counsels of maturity. It has a boundless confidence in itself.

I know no obstacle that surpasses the strength of the human mind, except truth.

The maxim has no need of it to prove itself. An argument demands an argument. The maxim is a law containing a set of arguments. An argument is complete in so far as it nears the maxim. Become maxim, its perfection rejects the proofs of the metamorphosis.⁷¹

Doubt is a homage paid to hope. It is not a voluntary homage. Hope would not consent to be merely a homage.

pas ce qu'il ne faut pas faire. Je chante ce qu'il faut faire. Le premier ne contient pas le second. Le second contient le premier.

La jeunesse écoute les conseils de l'âge mur. Elle a une confiance illimitée en elle-même.

Je ne connais pas d'obstacle qui passe les forces de l'esprit humain, sauf la vérité.

La maxime n'a pas besoin d'elle pour se prouver. Un raisonnement demande un raisonnement. La maxime est une loi qui renferme un ensemble de raisonnements. Un raisonnement se complète à mesure qu'il s'approche de la maxime. Devenu maxime, sa perfection rejette les preuves de la métamorphose.

Le doute est un hommage rendu à l'espoir. Ce n'est pas un hommage volontaire. L'espoir ne consentirait pas à n'être qu'un hommage.

Le mal s'insurge contre le bien. Il ne peut pas faire moins.

C'est une preuve d'amitié de ne pas s'apecevoir de l'augmentation de celle de nos amis.

L'amour n'est pas le bonheur.

Si nous n'avions point de défauts, nous ne prendrions pas tant de plaisir à nous corriger, à louer dans les autres ce qui nous manque.

Les hommes qui ont pris la résolution de détester leurs semblables ignorent qu'il faut commencer par se détester soi-même.

Les hommes qui ne se battent pas en duel croient que les hommes que se battent au duel à mort sont courageux.

Comme les turpitudes du roman s'accroupissent aux étalages! Pour un homme qui se perd, comme un autre pour une pièce de cent sous, il semble parfois qu'on tuerait un livre.

Lamartine a cru que la chute d'un ange deviendrait l'Elévation d'un Homme. Il a eu tort de le croire.

Pour faire servir le mal à la cause du bien, je dirai que l'intention du premier est mauvaise.

Une vérité banale renferme plus de génie que les ouvrages de Dickens, de Gustave Aymard, de Victor Hugo, de Landelle. Avec les derniers, un enfant, survivant à l'univers, ne pourrait pas reconstruire l'âme humaine. Avec la première, il le pourrait. Je suppose qu'il ne découvrît pas tôt ou tard la définition du sophisme.

Evil rebels against good. It cannot do less.

It is a proof of friendship to remain unconscious of the increase in that of our friends.[72]

Love is not happiness.

If we had no faults at all, we would not take such pleasure correcting ourselves, praising in others what we ourselves lack.[73]

Men who have resolved to hate their fellows do not know that one must begin by hating oneself.[74]

Men who do not fight duels believe that duellists to the death are brave.

How the depravities of the novel squat in shop windows! For a man who is lost, as was another for a five-franc piece,[75] it sometimes seems one might kill a book.

Lamartine believed that the fall of an angel[76] would become the Rise of a Man. He was wrong to believe it.

To make evil serve the cause of good I shall say that the former's intention is bad.

A banal truth contains more genius than the works of Dickens, Gustave Aymard, Victor Hugo, Landelle.[77] With these latter a child, surviving the universe, would not be able to reconstruct the human soul. With the former, he could. I presume that he would not sooner or later discover the definition of sophism.

Words which express evil are destined to take on a useful significance. Ideas change for the better. The meaning of words participates there.

Plagiarism is necessary. Progress implies it. It closely grasps an author's sentence, uses his expressions, deletes a false idea, replaces it with the right one.[78]

To be well made, a maxim does not call for correction. It calls for development.

As soon as dawn breaks, young girls go gathering roses. A gust of innocence sweeps through the valleys, the capitals, assists the intelligence of the most enthusiastic poets, showering down protection for cradles, wreaths for youth, belief in immortality for the aged.

I have seen men tire out moralists to lay bare their hearts,

Les mots qui expriment le mal sont destinés à prendre une signification d'utilité. Les idées s'améliorent. Le sens des mots y participe.

Le plagiat est nécessaire. Le progrès l'implique. Il serre de près la phrase d'un auteur, se sert de ses expressions, efface une idée fausse, la remplace par l'idée juste.

Une maxime, pour être bien faite, ne demande pas à être corrigée. Elle demande à être développée.

Dès que l'aurore a paru, les jeunes filles vont cueillir des roses. Un courant d'innocence parcourt les vallons, les capitales, secourt l'intelligence des poètes les plus enthousiastes, laisse tomber des protections pour les berceaux, des couronnes pour la jeunesse, des croyances à l'immortalité pour les vieillards.

J'ai vu les hommes lasser les moralistes à découvrir leur cœur, faire répandre sur eux la bénédiction d'en haut. Ils émettaient des méditations aussi vastes que possible, réjouissaient l'auteur de nos félicités. Ils respectaient l'enfance, la vieillesse, ce qui respire comme ce qui ne respire pas, rendaient hommage à la femme, consacraient à la pudeur les parties que le corps se réserve de nommer. Le firmament, dont j'admets la beauté, la terre, image de mon cœur, furent invoqués par moi, afin de me désigner un homme qui ne se crût pas bon. Le spectacle de ce monstre, s'il eût été réalisé, ne m'aurait pas fait mourir d'étonnement: on meurt à plus. Tout ceci se passe de commentaires.

La raison, le sentiment se conseillent, se suppléent. Quiconque ne connaît qu'un des deux, en renonçant à l'autre, se prive de la totalité des secours qui nous ont été accordés pour nous conduire. Vauvenargues a dit "se prive d'une partie des secours."

Quoique sa phrase, la mienne reposent sur les personnifications de l'âme dans le sentiment, la raison, celle que je choisirais au hasard ne serait pas meilleure que l'autre, si je les avais faites. L'une ne peut pas être rejetée par moi. L'autre a pu être acceptée de Vauvenargues.

Lorsqu'un prédécesseur emploie au bien un mot qui appartient au mal, il est dangereux que sa phrase subsiste à côté de l'autre. Il vaut mieux laisser au mot la signification du mal. Pour employer au

to have benediction scattered on them from above. They would utter meditations as expansive as possible, would gladden the author of our felicities. They respected childhood, old age, whatever breathes as well as what does not, would pay homage to womanhood and consecrate to modesty those parts which the body reserves the right to name. The firmament, whose beauty I admit, the earth, image of my heart, were invoked by me in order to find myself a man who did not believe himself virtuous. The sight of this monster, had it been realised, would not have made me die of astonishment: one dies for more than that. All this needs no comment.[79]

Reason, feeling, counsel and deputise for each other. Whoever knows only one of the two, by renouncing the other deprives himself of the totality of the aids which have been granted us for our guidance. Vauvenargues has said "deprives himself of part of the aid".[80]

Although his phrase and mine rest upon personifications of the soul in feeling, reason, the one I should choose at random would be no better than the other, had I coined them both. The one cannot be rejected by me. The other might have been accepted by Vauvenargues.

Whenever a predecessor uses in the sense of good a word that belongs to evil, it is dangerous for his phrase to exist beside the other. It is better to leave the word the evil meaning. To use in the sense of good a word belonging to evil, one must have the right to do so. He who uses for evil words belonging to the good does not possess it. He is not believed. No one would wish to wear Gérard de Nerval's necktie.[81]

The soul being one, sensibility, intelligence, will, reason, imagination, memory, may be introduced into the dissertation.

I had spent a long time studying the abstract sciences. The few people with whom I am in touch are not the kind to put me off these. When I began studying man I saw that these sciences are his own and that in exploring them I strayed less outside my province than others through their ignorance of them. I forgave them for not working at it at all! I did not expect to find many companions in the study of man. That is what is his alone. I was wrong. There are

bien un mot qui appartient au mal, il faut en avoir le droit. Celui qui emploie au mal les mots qui appartiennent au bien ne le possède pas. Il n'est pas cru. Personne ne voudrait se servir de la cravate de Gérard de Nerval.

L'âme étant une, l'on peut introduire dans le discours la sensibilité, l'intelligence, la volonté, la raison, l'imagination, la mémoire.

J'avais passé beaucoup de temps dans l'étude des sciences abstraites. Le peu de gens avec qui on communique n'était pas fait pour m'en dégoûter. Quand j'ai commencé l'étude de l'homme, j'ai vu que ces sciences lui sont propres, que je sortais moins de ma condition en y pénétrant que les autres en les ignorant. Je leur ai pardonné de ne s'y point appliquer! Je ne crus pas trouver beaucoup de compagnons dans l'étude de l'homme. C'est celle qui lui est propre. J'ai été trompé. Il y en a plus qui l'étudient que la géométrie.

Nous perdons la vie avec joie, pourvu qu'on n'en parle point.

Les passions diminuent avec l'âge. L'amour, qu'il ne faut pas classer parmi les passions, diminue de même. Ce qu'il perd d'un côté, il le regagne de l'autre. Il n'est plus sévère pour l'objet de ses vœux, se rendant justice à lui-même: l'expansion est acceptée. Les sens n'ont plus leur aiguillon pour exciter les sexes de la chair. L'amour de l'humanité commence. Dans ces jours où l'homme sent qu'il devient un autel que parent ses vertus, fait le compte de chaque douleur qui se releva, l'âme, dans un repli du cœur où tout semble prendre naissance, sent quelque chose qui ne palpite plus. J'ai nommé le souvenir.

L'écrivain, sans séparer l'une de l'autre, peut indiquer la loi qui régit chacune des ses poésies.

Quelques philosophes sont plus intelligents que quelques poètes. Spinoza, Malebranche, Aristote, Platon, ne sont pas Hégésippe Moreau, Malfilatre, Gilbert, André Chénier.

Faust, Manfred, Konrad, sont des types. Ce ne sont pas encore des types raisonnants. Ce sont déjà des types agitateurs.

Les descriptions sont une prairie, trois rhinocéros, la moitié d'un catafalque. Elles peuvent être le souvenir, la prophétie. Elles ne sont pas le paragraphe que je suis sur le point de terminer.

more studying him than geometry.[82]

We lose our lives joyfully, so long as we do not talk about it.[83]

Passions wane with age. Love, which must not be classed among the passions, wanes likewise. What it loses on the one hand it regains on the other. It is no longer strict with the object of its vows, doing itself justice: expansiveness is accepted. The senses no longer have their spur to excite the organs of the flesh. Love of humanity begins. On those days when man feels he has become an altar bedecked with his virtues and tots up every sorrow that revives, the soul, within the heart's inmost recess where everything seems to originate, feels something that no longer throbs. I referred to memory.[84]

The writer, without separating one from the other, can outline the law governing each of his poems.

Some philosophers are more intelligent than some poets. Spinoza, Malebranche, Aristotle, Plato are not Hégésippe Moreau, Malfilatre, Gilbert, André Chénier.[85]

Faust, Manfred, Conrad, are character types. They are not yet reasoning types. As it is, they are agitator types.

Descriptions are a meadow, three rhinoceroses, half a catafalque. They can be memory, prophecy. They are not the paragraph I am on the point of concluding.[86]

The governor of the soul is not the governor of a soul. The governor of a soul is the governor of the soul when these two kinds of soul are confused enough to be able to affirm that a governor is only a governess in the imagination of a jesting lunatic.[87]

The phenomenon passes. I seek laws.[88]

There are men who are not types. Types are not men. One must not let oneself be dominated by the accidental.

Judgements on poetry are of more value than poetry. They are the philosophy of poetry. Philosophy thus understood embodies poetry. Poetry could not do without philosophy. Philosophy could do without poetry.

Racine is not capable of condensing his tragedies into precepts. A tragedy is not a precept. To a like mind, a precept is a more intelligent action than a tragedy.

Le régulateur de l'âme n'est pas le régulateur d'une âme. Le régulateur d'une âme est le régulateur de l'âme, lorsque ces deux espèces d'âmes sont assez confondues pour pouvoir affirmer qu'un régulateur n'est une régulatrice que dans l'imagination d'un fou qui plaisante.

Le phénomène passe. Je cherche les lois.

Il y a des hommes qui ne sont pas des types. Les types ne sont pas des hommes. Il ne faut pas se laisser dominer par l'accidentel.

Les jugements sur la poésie ont plus de valeur que la poésie. Ils sont la philosophie de la poésie. La philosophie, ainsi comprise, englobe la poésie. La poésie ne pourra pas se passer de la philosophie. La philosophie pourra se passer de la poésie.

Racine n'est pas capable de condenser ses tragédies dans des préceptes. Une tragédie n'est pas un précepte. Pour un même esprit, un précepte est une action plus intelligente qu'une tragédie.

Mettez une plume d'oie dans la main d'un moraliste qui soit écrivain de premier ordre. Il sera supérieur aux poètes.

L'amour de la justice n'est, en la plupart des hommes, que le courage de souffrir l'injustice.

Cache-toi, guerre.

Les sentiments expriment le bonheur, font sourire. L'analyse des sentiments exprime le bonheur, toute personnalité mise à part; fait sourire. Les premiers élèvent l'âme, dépendamment de l'espace, de la durée, jusqu'à la conception de l'humanité, considérée en elle-même, dans ses membres illustres. La dernière élève l'âme, indépendamment de la durée, de l'espace, jusqu'à la conception de l'humanité, considérée dans son expression la plus haute, la volonté! Les premiers s'occupent des vices, des vertus; la dernière ne s'occupe que des vertus. Les sentiments ne connaissent pas l'ordre de leur marche. L'analyse des sentiments apprend à le faire connaître, augmente la vigueur des sentiments. Avec les premiers, tout est incertitude. Ils sont l'expression du bonheur, de la douleur, deux extrêmes. Avec la dernière, tout est certitude. Elle est l'expression de ce bonheur qui résulte, à un moment donné, de savoir se retenir, au milieu des passions bonnes ou mauvaises. Elle emploie son calme à fondre la description de ces passions dans un principe qui circule

Place a goose quill in the hand of a moralist who is a first-rate writer. He will be superior to the poets.

Love of justice is for most men only the courage to suffer injustice.[89]

Hide yourself, war.[90]

The feelings express happiness, make one smile. Analysis of the feelings expresses happiness, all personality aside; makes one smile. The former uplift the soul, dependent upon space, upon duration, up to the conception of humanity considered as itself, in its celebrated constituents! The latter uplifts the soul, independently of duration and space, up to the conception of humanity considered in its highest expression, the will! The former are concerned with vices and virtues; the latter only with virtues. Feelings do not know their marching order. The analysis of feelings teaches how to reveal it, increases the strength of the feelings. With the former, all is uncertainty. They are the expression of happiness, grief, two extremes. With the latter, all is certainty. It is the expression of that happiness which results at a given moment from knowing how to restrain oneself in the midst of good or evil passions. It uses its calm to render the description of the passions down to a principle which flows through the pages: the non-existence of evil. The feelings weep when they must, as when they need not. Analysis of the feelings does not weep. It possesses a latent sensibility which catches one off guard, prevails over miseries, teaches how to dispense with a guide, provides a combat weapon. The feelings, sign of weakness, are not feeling! The analysis of feeling, sign of strength, generates the most magnificent feelings I know. The writer who is taken in by feelings must not be placed on a par with the writer who is taken in neither by feelings nor himself. Youth intends sentimental lucubrations. Maturity begins to reason without confusion. He was only feeling, he thinks. He used to let his sensations wander: now he gives them a pilot. If I liken humanity to a woman, I shall not expatiate upon her youth's being on the wane and the approach of her middle-age. Her mind changes for the better. Her ideal of poetry will change. Tragedies, poems, elegies will no longer take precedence. The coolness of the maxim shall prevail! In Quin-

à travers les pages: la non-existence du mal. Les sentiments pleurent quand il le leur faut, comme quand il ne le leur faut pas. L'analyse des sentiments ne pleure pas. Elle possède une sensibilité latente, qui prend au dépourvu, emporte au-dessus des misères, apprend à se passer de guide, fournit une arme de combat. Les sentiments, marque de la faiblesse, ne sont pas le sentiment! L'analyse du sentiment, marque de la force, engendre les sentiments les plus magnifiques que je connaisse. L'écrivain qui se laisse tromper par les sentiments ne doit pas être mis en ligne de compte avec l'écrivain qui ne se laisse tromper ni par les sentiments, ni par lui-même. La jeunesse se propose des élucubrations sentimentales. L'âge mur commence à raisonner sans trouble. Il ne faisait que sentir, il pense. Il laissait vagabonder ses sensations: voici qu'il leur donne un pilote. Si je considère l'humanité comme une femme, je ne développerai pas que sa jeunesse est à son déclin, que son âge mûr s'approche. Son esprit change dans le sens du mieux. L'idéal de sa poésie changera. Les tragédies, les poëmes, les élégies ne primeront plus. Primera la froideur de la maxime! Du temps de Quinault, l'on aurait été capable de comprendre ce que je viens de dire. Grâce à quelques lueurs, éparses, depuis quelques années, dans les revues, les in-folios, j'en suis capable moi-même. Le genre que j'entreprends est aussi différent du genre des moralistes, qui ne font que constater le mal, sans indiquer le remède, que ce dernier ne l'est pas des mélodrames, des oraisons funèbres, de l'ode, de la stance religieuse. Il n'y a pas le sentiment des luttes.

Elohim est fait à l'image de l'homme.

Plusieurs choses certaines sont contredites. Plusieurs choses fausses sont incontredites. La contradiction est la marque de la fausseté. L'incontradiction est la marque de la certitude.

Une philosophie pour les sciences existe. Il n'en existe pas pour la poésie. Je ne connais pas de moraliste qui soit poète de premier ordre. C'est étrange, dira quelqu'un.

C'est une chose horrible de sentir s'écouler ce qu'on possède. L'on ne s'y attache même qu'avec l'idée de chercher s'il n'a point quelque chose de permanent.

L'homme est un sujet vide d'erreurs. Tout lui montre la vérité.

ault's[91] time they could have understood what I have just said. Thanks to some scattered glimmers during the last few years from magazines and folios, I can do so myself. The style I adopt differs as much from that of the moralists, who only record evil without prescribing the remedy, as the latter's does not from melodramas, funeral orations, the ode, the devotional stanza. There is no sense of struggle.

Elohim is made in the image of man.[92]

A number of certainties are contradicted. A number of falsehoods are uncontradicted. Contradiction is the sign of falsity. Noncontradiction is the sign of certitude.[93]

A philosophy for the sciences exists. It does not exist for poetry. I know of no moralist who is a first-rate poet. That's odd, someone will say.

It is a horrible thing to feel what one possesses slip away. One devotes oneself only to the idea of trying to find out whether anything at all is permanent.[94]

Man is a subject devoid of fallacies. Everything shows him the truth. Nothing deludes him. The two principles of truth, reason and sense, apart from the fact that they do not lack sincerity, enlighten one another. The senses make reason clearer through real appearances. The same service they render it, they receive from it. Each takes its revenge. The soul's phenomena appease the senses, make impressions upon them which I do not guarantee to be troublesome. They do not lie. They do not vie with each other in making mistakes.[95]

Poetry should be made by all. Not by one. Poor Hugo! Poor Racine! Poor Coppée! Poor Corneille! Poor Boileau! Poor Scarron! Tics, tics, and tics.[96]

The sciences have two extremities which meet. The first is the ignorance in which men find themselves at birth. The second is that attained by great souls. They have surveyed whatever man can know, find that they know all, meet in that same ignorance whence they started. It is a clever ignorance, which knows itself. Those among them who, having emerged from the first ignorance, have been unable to achieve the other and have some smattering of this

Rien ne l'abuse. Les deux principes de la vérité, raison, sens, outre qu'ils ne manquent pas de sincérité, s'éclaircissent l'un l'autre. Les sens éclaircissent la raison par des apparences vraies. Ce même service qu'ils lui font, ils la reçoivent d'elle. Chacun prend sa revanche. Les phénomènes de l'âme pacifient les sens, leur font des impressions que je ne garantis pas fâcheuses. Ils ne mentent pas. Ils ne se trompent pas à l'envi.

La poésie doit être faite par tous. Non par un. Pauvre Hugo! Pauvre Racine! Pauvre Coppée! Pauvre Corneille! Pauvre Boileau! Pauvre Scarron! Tics, tics, et tics.

Les sciences ont deux extrémités qui se touchent. La première est l'ignorance où se trouvent les hommes en naissant. La deuxième est celle qu'atteignent les grandes âmes. Elles ont parcouru ce que les hommes peuvent savoir, trouvent qu'ils savent tout, se rencontrent dans cette même ignorance d'où ils étaient partis. C'est une ignorance savante, qui se connaît. Ceux d'entre eux qui, étant sortis de la première ignorance, n'ont pu arriver à l'autre, ont quelque teinture de cette science suffisante, font les entendus. Ceux-là ne troublent pas le monde, ne jugent pas plus mal de tout que les autres. Le peuple, les habiles composent le train d'une nation. Les autres, qui la respectent, n'en sont pas moins respectés.

Pour savoir les choses, il ne faut pas en savoir le détail. Comme il est fini, nos connaissances sont solides.

L'amour ne se confond pas avec la poésie.

La femme est à mes pieds!

Pour décrire le ciel, il ne faut pas y transporter les matériaux de la terre. Il faut laisser la terre, ses matériaux, là où ils sont, afin d'embellir la vie par son idéal. Tutoyer Elohim, lui adresser la parole, est une bouffonnerie qui n'est pas convenable. Le meilleur moyen d'être reconnaissant envers lui, n'est pas de lui corner aux oreilles qu'il est puissant, qu'il a créé le monde, que nous sommes des vermiceaux en comparaison de sa grandeur. Il le sait mieux que nous. Les hommes peuvent se dispenser de le lui apprendre. Le meilleur moyen d'être reconnaissant envers lui est de consoler l'humanité, de rapporter tout à elle, de la prendre par la main, de la traiter en frère. C'est plus vrai.

self-satisfied knowledge, pose as experts. The latter do not disturb people, are no more mistaken in their judgements on everything than others. The masses, the skilled, make up the retinue of a nation. The others, who respect it,[97] are equally respected by it.[98]

To know things, one need not know their details.[99] As detail is finite, our cognitions are sound.

Love does not confuse itself with poetry.[100]

Woman is at my feet! [101]

To describe heaven it is not necessary to transport the materials of earth there. One must leave earth and its materials where they are, so as to beautify life with its ideal. To address Elohim familiarly is an unseemly buffoonery. The best way of showing him gratitude is not by yelling in his ears that he is mighty, that he created the world, that we are worms compared to his greatness. He knows it better than we. Men may excuse themselves from informing him of that. The best way of showing him gratitude is to console humanity, to restore all to it, take it by the hand and treat it like a brother. This is more genuine.

To study order, it is not necessary to study disorder. Scientific experiments, like tragedies, stanzas to my sister,[102] the gibberish of misfortunes, have no business here below.

Not all laws are fit to mention.

To study evil so as to bring out the good is not to study good in itself. Given a suitable phenomenon, I shall seek its cause.

Until now, misfortune has been described so as to inspire pity and terror.[103] I shall describe happiness so as to inspire their opposites.

A logic exists for poetry. It is not the same as that of philosophy. Philosophers are not so numerous as poets. The poets have the right to consider themselves above the philosophers.[104]

I need not bother about what I shall do later. I ought to do what I am doing. I need not discover whatever things I shall come across later. In the new science, everything takes its time, such is its excellence.

There is the stuff of the poet in the moralists and philosophers. The poets include the thinker. Each caste suspects the other, deve-

Pour étudier l'ordre, il ne faut pas étudier le désordre. Les expériences scientifiques, comme les tragédies, les stances à ma sœur, le galimatias des infortunes n'ont rien à faire ici-bas.

Toutes les lois ne sont pas bonnes à dire.

Etudier le mal, pour faire sortir le bien, n'est pas étudier le bien en lui-même. Un phénomène bon étant donné, je chercherai sa cause.

Jusqu'à présent, l'on a décrit le malheur, pour inspirer la terreur, la pitié. Je décrirai le bonheur pour inspirer leurs contraires.

Une logique existe pour la poésie. Ce n'est pas la même que celle de la philosophie. Les philosophes ne sont pas autant que les poètes. Les poètes ont le droit de se considérer au-dessus des philosophes.

Je n'ai pas besoin de m'occuper de ce que je ferai plus tard. Je devais faire ce que je fais. Je n'ai pas besoin de découvrir quelles choses je découvrirai plus tard. Dans la nouvelle science, chaque chose vient à son tour, telle est son excellence.

Il y a de l'étoffe du poète dans les moralistes, les philosophes. Les poètes renferment le penseur. Chaque caste soupçonne l'autre, développe ses qualités au détriment de celles qui la rapprochent de l'autre caste. La jalousie des premiers ne veut pas avouer que les poètes sont plus forts qu'elle. L'orgueil des derniers se déclare incompétent à rendre justice à des cervelles plus tendres. Quelle que soit l'intelligence d'un homme, il faut que le procédé de penser soit le même pour tous.

L'existence des tics étant constatée, que l'on ne s'étonne pas de voir les mêmes mots revenir plus souvent qu'à leur tour: dans Lamartine, les pleurs qui tombent des naseaux de son cheval, la couleur des cheveux de sa mère; dans Hugo, l'ombre et le détraqué, font partie de la reliure.

La science que j'entreprends est une science distincte de la poésie. Je ne chante pas cette dernière. Je m'efforce de découvrir sa source. A travers le gouvernail qui dirige toute pensée poétique, les professeurs de billard distingueront le développement des thèses sentimentales.

Le théorème est railleur de sa nature. Il n'est pas indécent. Le

lops its qualities to the detriment of those which bring it nearer the other caste. The jealousy of the former does not want to admit that the poets are stronger than they. The pride of the latter declares itself unqualified to do justice to more sensitive brains. Whatever a man's intelligence may be, the process of thought must be the same for all.

The existence of tics having been established, let none be surprised to see the same words recur more than their fair share: in Lamartine, the tears which fall down his horse's nostrils,[105] the colour of his mother's hair;[106] in Hugo, the darkness and the broken man; these are part of the binding.

The science I undertake is a science distinct from poetry. I do not sing of the latter. I strive to discover its source. Through the rudder that steers all poetic thought, billiards professors will discern the evolution of sentimental theses.

The theorem is mocking by nature, it is not indecent. The theorem does not ask to be allowed to serve as application. The application made of it belittles the theorem, turns it indecent. Call the application the struggle against matter, against the ravages of the spirit.[107]

To struggle against evil is to do it too much honour. If I allow men to despise it, let them not fail to say that this is all I can do for them.

Man is certain not to be wrong.

We are not content with the life we have in us. We want to live in the idea others have of an imaginary life. We do our utmost to appear as we are. We exert ourselves to preserve this imaginary being, which is none other than the real one. If we have generosity, fidelity, we are eager not to let it be known, so as to attach these virtues to that being. We do not detach them from ourselves in order to join them to it. We are brave so as to acquire the reputation of not being poltroons. Sign of our being's capacity not to be satisfied with one without the other, to renounce neither one nor the other. The man who did not live for preserving his valour would be infamous.[108]

Despite the sight of our splendours, that grasp us by the

théorème ne demande pas à servir d'application. L'application qu' on en fait rabaisse le théorème, se rend indécente. Appelez la lutte contre la matière, contre les ravages de l'esprit, application.

Lutter contre le mal, est lui faire trop d'honneur. Si je permets aux hommes de le mépriser, qu'ils ne manquent pas de dire que c'est tout ce que je puis faire pour eux.

L'homme est certain de ne pas se tromper.

Nous ne nous contentons pas de la vie que nous avons en nous. Nous voulons vivre dans l'idée des autres d'une vie imaginaire. Nous nous efforçons de paraître tels que nous sommes. Nous travaillons à conserver cet être imaginaire, qui n'est autre chose que le véritable. Si nous avons la générosité, la fidélité, nous nous empressons de ne pas le faire savoir, afin d'attacher ces vertus à cet être. Nous ne les détachons pas de nous pour les y joindre. Nous sommes vaillants pour acquérir la réputation de ne pas être poltrons. Marque de la capacité de notre être de ne pas être satisfait de l'un sans l'autre, de ne renoncer ni à l'un ni à l'autre. L'homme qui ne vivrait pas pour conserver sa vertu serait infâme.

Malgré la vue de nos grandeurs, qui nous tient à la gorge, nous avons un instinct qui nous corrige, que nous ne pouvons réprimer, qui nous élève!

La nature a des perfections pour montrer qu'elle est l'image d'Elohim, des défauts pour montrer qu'elle n'en est pas moins que l'image.

Il est bon qu'on obéisse aux lois. Le peuple comprend ce qui les rend justes. On ne les quitte pas. Quand on fait dépendre leur justice d'autre chose, il est aisé de la rendre douteuse. Les peuples ne sont pas sujets à se révolter.

Ceux qui sont dans le déréglement disent à ceux qui sont dans l'ordre que ce sont eux qui s'éloignent de la nature. Ils croient le suivre. Il faut avoir un point fixe pour juger. Où ne trouverons-nous pas ce point dans la morale?

Rien n'est moins étrange que les contrariétés que l'on découvre dans l'homme. Il est fait pour connaître la vérité. Il la cherche. Quand il tâche de la saisir, il s'éblouit, se confond de telle sorte, qu'il ne donne pas sujet à lui en disputer la possession. Les uns

throat, we have an instinct which sets us to rights, which we cannot repress, which uplifts us![109]

Nature has perfections to show that she is the image of Elohim, defects to show that she is his image none the less.[110]

It is fitting to obey the laws. The people understand what makes them just. One does not abandon them. When one makes their justice subject to something else, it is easy to render it doubtful. The people are not liable to revolt.[111]

Those who are in disorder tell those who are orderly that it is they who are deviating from nature. They believe themselves to be following it. A fixed point is needed in order to judge. Where in morality do we not find this point?[112]

Nothing is less strange than the contrarieties one detects in man. He is made to know the truth. He seeks it. When he tries to grasp it he is dazzled, is disconcerted so that he gives no cause for disputing with him for possession of it. Some wish to rob man of the knowledge of truth, others want to assure him of it. Each works from such dissimilar motives that man's perplexity is destroyed. He has no light other than the one he finds in his character.[113]

We are born just. Everyone inclines towards himself. It is towards order. One must incline towards the general. The inclination towards the self is the end of all disorder, in war, in the economy.[114]

Men, having contrived to recover from death, misery, ignorance, in order to make themselves happy took it upon themselves not to think about that at all. This is all they have been able to devise as consolation for so few ills. Ultra-rich consolation. It doesn't go far towards curing evil. It hides it for a short while and by hiding it ensures that we think about curing it. Through a legitimate inversion of man's nature, boredom, his most palpable evil, does not happen to be his greatest good. It may contribute more than anything else to making him seek his cure. That is all. Diversion, which he regards as his greatest good, is his most insignificant evil. It brings him closer than anything to seeking the remedy for his ills. Both are counter-proofs of the misery, of the corruption of man, but for his greatness. Man is bored, seeks out this host of occupations. He

veulent ravir à l'homme la connaissance de la vérité, les autres veulent la lui assurer. Chacun emploie des motifs si dissemblables, qu'ils détruisent l'embarras de l'homme. Il n'a pas d'autre lumière que celle qui se trouve dans sa nature.

Nous naissons justes. Chacun tend à soi. C'est envers l'ordre. Il faut tendre au général. La pente vers soi est la fin de tout désordre, en guerre, en économie.

Les hommes, ayant pu guérir de la mort, de la misère, de l'ignorance, se sont avisés, pour se rendre heureux, de n'y point penser. C'est tout ce qu'ils ont pu inventer pour se consoler de si peu de maux. Consolation richissime. Elle ne va pas à guérir le mal. Elle le cache pour un peu de temps. En le cachant, elle fait qu'on pense à le guérir. Par un légitime renversement de la nature de l'homme, il ne se trouve pas que l'ennui, qui est son mal le plus sensible, soit son plus grand bien. Il peut contribuer plus que toutes choses à lui faire chercher sa guérison. Voilà tout. Le divertissement, qu'il regarde comme son plus grand bien, est son plus infime mal. Il le rapproche plus que toutes choses de chercher le remède à ses maux. L'un et l'autre sont une contre-preuve de la misère, de la corruption de l'homme, hormis de sa grandeur. L'homme s'ennuie, cherche cette multitude d'occupations. Il a l'idée du bonheur qu'il a gagné; lequel trouvant en soi, il le cherche, dans les choses extérieures. Il se contente. Le malheur n'est ni dans nous, ni dans les créatures. Il est en Elohim.

La nature nous rendant heureux en tous états, nos désirs nous figurent un état malheureux. Ils joignent à l'état où nous sommes les peines de l'état où nous ne sommes pas. Quand nous arriverions à ces peines, nous ne serions pas malheureux pour cela, nous aurions d'autres désirs conformes à un nouvel état.

La force de la raison paraît mieux en ceux qui la connaissent qu'en ceux qui ne la connaissent pas.

Nous sommes si peu présomptueux que nous voudrions être connus de la terre, même des gens qui viendront quand nous n'y serons plus. Nous sommes si peu vains, que l'estime de cinq personnes, mettons six, nous amuse, nous honore.

Peu de chose nous console. Beaucoup de chose nous afflige.

has an idea of the happiness he has won; finding this within himself, he looks for it in outward things. He is content. Misfortune is neither in us nor in other creatures. It is in Elohim.[115]

Nature making us happy in all circumstances, our desires depict for us an unhappy state. They join to the state in which we are the afflictions of the state in which we are not. When we came to these afflictions we would not be unhappy because of that; we would have other desires consonant with a new state.[116]

The strength of reason is better apparent in those who understand it than in those who do not.[117]

We have so little presumption that we should like to be known in the world, even to those who come after when we are no more. We have so little vanity that the esteem of five people, say six, amuses us, does us honour.[118]

Few things console us. Many things afflict us.[119]

Modesty is so natural in man's heart that a workman takes care not to boast, wants to have his admirers. Philosophers want them. Poets above all! Those who write in favour of glory want to have the glory of having written well. Those who read it want to have the glory of having read it. I, who write this, pride myself on having this desire. Those who read it will make a similar boast.[120]

The inventions of man go on increasing. The kindness, the malice of people in general does not remain the same.[121]

The mind of the greatest man is not so dependent that it should be caused disquiet by the slightest noise of the *Tintamarre* going on around him.[122] The silence of a cannon is not required to impede his thoughts. The noise of a weathercock or a pulley is not necessary. The fly[123] is not reasoning well just now. A man buzzes at its ears. This is enough to render it incapable of good advice. If I would have it find truth, I should chase away this animal which holds its reason in check and disquiets that intelligence which governs kingdoms.

The object of those people who play tennis with such mental concentration, such physical activity, is to boast to their friends that they have played better than someone else. It is the source of their assiduity. Some toil in their chambers to show the scholars

La modestie est si naturelle dans le cœur de l'homme, qu'un ouvrier a soin de ne pas se vanter, veut avoir ses admirateurs. Les philosophes en veulent. Les poètes surtout! Ceux qui écrivent en faveur de la gloire veulent avoir la gloire d'avoir bien écrit. Ceux qui le lisent veulent avoir la gloire de l'avoir lu. Moi, qui écris ceci, je me vante d'avoir cette envie. Ceux qui le liront se vanteront de même.

Les inventions des hommes vont en augmentant. La bonté, la malice du monde en général ne reste pas la même.

L'esprit du plus grand homme n'est pas si dépendant, qu'il soit sujet à être troublé par le moindre bruit du Tintamarre, qui se fait autour de lui. Il ne faut pas le silence d'un canon pour empêcher ses pensées. Il ne faut pas le bruit d'une girouette, d'une poulie. La mouche ne raisonne pas bien à présent. Un homme bourdonne à ses oreilles. C'en est assez pour la rendre incapable de bon conseil. Si je veux qu'elle puisse trouver la vérité, je chasserai cet animal qui tient sa raison en échec, trouble cette intelligence qui gouverne les royaumes.

L'objet de ces gens qui jouent à la paume avec tant d'application d'esprit, d'agitation de corps, est celui de se vanter avec leurs amis qu'ils ont mieux joué qu'un autre. C'est la source de leur attachement. Les uns suent dans leurs cabinets pour montrer aux savants qu'ils ont résolu une question d'algèbre qui ne l'avait pu être jusqu'ici. Les autres s'exposent aux périls, pour se vanter d'une place qu'ils auraient prise moins spirituellement, à mon gré. Les derniers se tuent pour remarquer ces choses. Ce n'est pas pour en devenir moins sages. C'est surtout pour montrer qu'ils en connaissent la solidité. Ceux-là sont les moins sots de la bande. Ils le sont avec connaissance. On peut penser des autres qu'ils ne le seraient pas, s'ils n'avaient pas cette connaissance.

L'exemple de la chasteté d'Alexandre n'a pas fait plus de continents que celui de son ivrognerie a fait de tempérants. On n'a pas de honte de n'être pas aussi vertueux que lui. On croit n'être pas tout à fait dans les vertus du commun des hommes, quand on se voit dans les vertus de ces grands hommes. On tient à eux par le bout par où ils tiennent au peuple. Quelque élevés qu'ils soient, ils

that they have resolved a hitherto insoluble algebraic problem. Others expose themselves to dangers so as to boast of a place they would have found for themselves less wittily, to my mind. The latter kill themselves in order to note these things. Not in order to become the less wise for them. It is above all to show that they understand the substantiality of them. These are the least stupid of the bunch. They are so advisedly. One may consider that the others would not be, if they did not have this understanding.[124]

The example of Alexander's chastity made no more celibates than that of his drunkenness made teetotallers. One is not ashamed not to be as virtuous as he. One can believe oneself not quite within the virtues of the majority of mankind when one sees oneself within the virtues of these great men. One values them by how they adhere to the people. However noble they may be, they are united with the rest of mankind in some aspect. They are not suspended in the air, separated from our society. If they are greater than we, it is because their feet are held as high as ours. They are all on the same level, rest upon the same earth. By this extremity they are as exalted as we, as children, a little more than the beasts.[125]

The best way to persuade consists of not persuading.[126]

Despair is the least of our errors.[127]

When a thought presents itself to us like a truth generally current and we take the trouble to develop it, we find that it is a discovery.[128]

One can be just, if one is not human.[129]

The storms of youth precede brilliant days.[130]

Unconsciousness, dishonour, lewdness, hate, men's scorn, are to be had for money. Liberality multiplies the advantages of riches.[131]

Those who have integrity in their pleasures, have sincerity in their business. It is the sign of a mild disposition when pleasure makes one human.[132]

The moderation of great men limits only their virtues.[133]

It is offensive to human beings to give them praise that extends the bounds of their merit. Many people are modest enough to suffer appreciation willingly.[134]

sont unis au reste des hommes par quelque endroit. Ils ne sont pas suspendus en l'air, séparés de notre société. S'ils sont plus grands que nous, c'est qu'ils ont les pieds aussi haut que les nôtres. Ils sont tous à même niveau, s'appuient sur la même terre. Par cette extrémité, ils sont aussi relevés que nous, que les enfants, un peu plus que les bêtes.

Le meilleur moyen de persuader consiste à ne pas persuader.

Le désespoir est la plus petite de nos erreurs.

Lorsqu'une pensée s'offre à nous comme une vérité qui court les rues, que nous prenons la peine de la développer, nous trouvons que c'est une découverte.

On peut être juste, si l'on n'est pas humain.

Les orages de la jeunesse précèdent les jours brillants.

L'inconscience, le déshonneur, la lubricité, la haine, le mépris des hommes sont à prix d'argent. La libéralité multiplie les avantages des richesses.

Ceux qui ont de la probité dans leurs plaisirs en ont une sincère dans leurs affaires. C'est la marque d'un naturel peu féroce, lorsque le plaisir rend humain.

La modération des grands hommes ne borne que leurs vertus.

C'est offenser les humains que de leur donner les louanges qui élargissent les bornes de leur mérite. Beaucoup de gens sont assez modeste pour souffrir sans peine qu'on les apprécie.

Il faut tout attendre, rien craindre du temps, des hommes.

Si le mérite, la gloire ne rendent pas les hommes malheureux, ce qu'on appelle malheur ne mérite pas leurs regrets. Une âme daigne accepter la fortune, le repos, s'il leur faut superposer la vigueur de ses sentiments, l'essor de son génie.

On estime les grands desseins, lorsqu'on se sent capable des grands succès.

La réserve est l'apprentissage des esprits.

On dit des choses solides, lorsqu'on ne cherche pas à en dire d'extraordinaires.

Rien n'est faux qui soit vrai; rien n'est vrai qui soit faux. Tout est le contraire de songe, de mensonge.

Il ne faut pas croire que ce que la nature a fait aimable soit

We must expect everything, fear nothing, from time and men.[135]

If talent, fame, do not make men unhappy, what one calls misfortune does not merit their regrets. A soul condescends to accept fortune, tranquillity, if they must superpose the strength of its feelings, the full scope of its genius.[136]

One respects great plans, when one feels capable of great successes.[137]

Reserve is the apprenticeship of consciousness.[138]

We say sound things when we do not strive to say extraordinary ones.[139]

Nothing true is false: nothing false is true. Everything is the contrary of dream, of untruth.[140]

We must not believe that what nature has created amiable is vicious. There has been no century, no nation, that has established imaginary virtues, vices.[141]

One can judge the beauty of life only by that of death.[142]

A dramatist can give the word passion a useful meaning. He is no longer a dramatist. A moralist gives any word at all a useful meaning. He is still the moralist![143]

Whoever contemplates the life of a man therein finds the history of the species. Nothing has been able to make it evil.[144]

Must I write in verse to separate myself from other men? Let charity decide![145]

The pretext of those who make others happy is that they wish them well.[146]

Generosity enjoys the happiness of others, as though it were responsible for it.[147]

Order prevails in the human race. Reason, virtue, are not the most powerful there.[148]

Princes create few ingrates. They give all they can.[149]

One can wholeheartedly love those in whom one recognises great shortcomings. It would be impertinence to believe that imperfection alone has the right to please us. Our weaknesses bind us to each other as much as that which is not virtue could.[150]

If our friends do us services, we think that as friends they owe

vicieux. Il n'y a pas de siècle, de peuple qui ait établi des vertus, des vices imaginaires.

On ne peut juger de la beauté de la vie que par celle de la mort.

Un dramaturge peut donner au mot passion une signification d'utilité. Ce n'est plus un dramaturge. Un moraliste donne à n'importe quel mot une signification d'utilité. C'est encore le moraliste!

Qui considère la vie d'un homme y trouve l'histoire du genre. Rien n'a pu le rendre mauvais.

Faut-il que j'écrive en vers pour me séparer des autres hommes? Que la charité prononce!

Le prétexte de ceux qui font le bonheur des autres est qu'ils veulent leur bien.

La générosité jouit des félicités d'autrui, comme si elle en était responsable.

L'ordre domine dans le genre humain. La raison, la vertu n'y sont pas les plus fortes.

Les princes font peu d'ingrats. Ils donnent tout ce qu'ils peuvent.

On peut aimer de tout son cœur ceux en qui on reconnaît de grands défauts. Il y aurait de l'impertinence à croire que l'imperfection a seule le droit de nous plaire. Nos faiblesses nous attachent les uns aux autres autant que pourrait le faire ce qui n'est pas la vertu.

Si nos amis nous rendent des services, nous pensons qu'à titre d'amis ils nous les doivent. Nous ne pensons pas du tout qu'ils nous doivent leur inimitié.

Celui qui serait né pour commander, commanderait jusque sur le trône.

Lorsque les devoirs nous ont épuisés, nous croyons avoir épuisé les devoirs. Nous disons que tout peut remplir le cœur de l'homme.

Tout vit par l'action. De là, communication des êtres, harmonie de l'univers. Cette loi si féconde de la nature, nous trouvons que c'est un vice dans l'homme. Il est obligé d'y obéir. Ne pouvant subsister dans le repos, nous concluons qu'il est à sa place.

On sait ce que sont le soleil, les cieux. Nous avons le secret de leurs mouvements. Dans la main d'Elohim, instrument aveugle,

us them. We do not think at all that they owe us their enmity.[151]

He who is born to command would command even on the throne.[152]

When duties have exhausted us, we think we have exhausted duties. We say that everything can fill the heart of man.[153]

Everything lives by action. Hence communication between beings, harmony of the universe. This natural law, so fertile, we find to be a vice in man. He is obliged to obey it. We conclude that, not being able to exist in repose, he is in his place.[154]

One knows what the sun, the heavens are. We have the secrets of their movements. In Elohim's hand, blind instrument, insentient spring, the world attracts our tributes. The revolutions of empires, the faces of the times, the nations, the conquerors of science, this is the result of a crawling atom which lasts but a day, destroys the spectacle of the universe throughout all ages.[155]

There are more truths than delusions, more good qualities than bad, more pleasures than pains. We like to control character. We raise ourselves above our kind. We enrich ourselves by the consideration which we shower upon it. We do not believe we can separate our own interest from that of humanity, nor slander the race without compromising ourselves. This ridiculous vanity has filled books with hymns on nature's behalf. Man is in disgrace with those who think. They vie with each other in burdening him with fewer vices. When was he not on the point of uplifting himself, of having his virtues reinstated?[156]

Nothing has been said. It is too soon since the more than seven thousand years that there have been men. With regard to morals, as with all else, the least good is exalted. We have the advantage of working after the ancients, the skilful ones among the moderns.[157]

We are capable of friendship, justice, compassion, reason. O my friends! what then is the absence of virtue?[158]

As long as my friends do not die, I shall not speak of death.[159]

We are dismayed by our relapses, by seeing that our misfortunes have been able to cure us of our defects.[160]

One can judge the beauty of death only by that of life.[161]

ressort insensible, le monde attire nos hommages. Les révolutions des empires, les faces des temps, les nations, les conquérants de la science, cela vient d'un atôme qui rampe, ne dure qu'un jour, détruit le spectacle de l'univers dans tous les âges.

Il y a plus de vérité que d'erreurs, plus de bonnes qualités que de mauvaises, plus de plaisirs que de peines. Nous aimons à contrôler le caractère. Nous nous élevons au-dessus de notre espèce. Nous nous enrichissons de la considération dont nous la comblâmes. Nous croyons ne pas pouvoir séparer notre intérêt de celui de l'humanité, ne pas médire du genre sans nous commettre nous-mêmes. Cette vanité ridicule a rempli les livres d'hymnes en faveur de la nature. L'homme est en disgrâce chez ceux qui pensent. C'est à qui le chargera de moins de vices. Quand ne fut-il pas sur le point de se relever, de se faire restituer ses vertus?

Rien n'est dit. L'on vient trop tôt depuis plus de sept mille ans qu'il y a des hommes. Sur ce qui concerne les mœurs, comme sur le reste, le moins bon est enlevé. Nous avons l'avantage de travailler après les anciens, les habiles d'entre les modernes.

Nous sommes susceptibles d'amitié, de justice, de compassion, de raison. O mes amis! qu'est-ce donc que l'absence de vertu?

Tant que mes amis ne mourront pas, je ne parlerai pas de la mort.

Nous sommes consternés de nos rechutes, de voir que nos malheurs ont pu nous corriger de nos défauts.

On ne peut juger de la beauté de la mort que par celle de la vie.

Les trois points terminateurs me font hausser les épaules de pitié. A-t-on besoin de cela pour prouver que l'on est un homme d'esprit, c'est-à-dire un imbécile? Comme si la clarté ne valait pas le vague, à propos de points!

The three terminational points[162] make me shrug my shoulders in pity. Does one need that to prove one is a wit, in other words an imbecile? As if clarity were not as good as vacancy, on the subject of points![163]

ANNOUNCEMENT[164]

This continuing publication has no price. Each subscriber decides upon his subscription for himself. He gives, moreover, only what he wants.

Persons receiving the first two instalments are requested not to refuse them, under any pretext whatever.

COMPLIMENTS:
The Editor
I.D.
Rue du Faubourg-Montmartre 7.

Notes to Poésies

1. The dedicatees:

Alexis-Edouard-Georges Dazet (1852-1920). Mentioned by name frequently in first version of *Chant* 1. All references to him thereafter deleted, he metamorphoses into octopus, toad, *acarus sarcoptes* and other Maldororian fauna. He and Ducasse knew each other during 1861-2 at the Tarbes lycée. Dazet was called to the bar at Tarbes, then Paris. Thrice married, with several children, one of whom died in the 1914-18 war. Freemason with left-wing sympathies. Struck off bar at Tunis (1896) for unspecified reasons. Stood unsuccessfully in local elections and published left-wing pamphlets. Involved in business scandal in Tarbes area, 1908. Magistrate at Monzols (Rhône), 1912. André Breton visited his widow, but apparently no papers or reminiscences of Ducasse could be found in the house of this, perhaps his closest, friend.

Henri Mue. Clever student, son of a businessman from St Denis (Seine). A long way from home to study in Tarbes, as Caradec (op. cit.) points out. At his death Head of Tax Department at Toulouse.

Pedro Zurmaran. ("Zumaran" is a misspelling.) Came from doctor's family in Montevideo. Not a school contemporary, his friendship with Ducasse probably dates from Ducasse's second stay in Montevideo, 1867.

Nothing is known of *Louis Durcour* or *Joseph Durand*. Neither was a school friend of Ducasse. The latter rumoured to have participated in the Commune and to have left France without further trace.

Joseph Bleumstein. Student of this name from Buenos Aires entered Pau lycée in 1866, after Ducasse had left and was probably living at Tarbes. Ducasse would therefore have been considerably older.

Paul Lespès (1847-1928). Ducasse's contemporary at Pau lycée and the only one to have left direct reminiscences of him (see pp.136-41). Headed second group of dedicatees – they were ranged not in convenient alphabetical order but perhaps in descending degrees of intimacy – that of the "fellow-students". Lawyer, magistrate, appeal court judge at Pau. Died near Bayonne.

Georges Minvielle. Also at Pau lycée. Clever student, who became lawyer then magistrate. Died at Pau, 1923 (see also pp.136.41).

Auguste Delmas. Born at Tarbes. At Pau lycée. Two forms ahead of Ducasse. Made career in law.

Alfred Sircos. Editor-publisher of *La Jeunesse* (1868-9) and *L'Union des Jeunes* (1869-70). Both he and Damé, as Faurisson (op. cit.) notes, seem to have been highly serious, earnest young men. Sircos's real name was Emion, his pseudonym Epistémon (see review of *Chant 1*, p.145).

Frédéric Damé (1849-1907). Born at Tonnerre. Law studies in Paris. Founded magazine that was closed down, *L'Avenir Littéraire*. Associated with Romanian revolutionaries in Paris. Contributor to many newspapers and periodicals. In 1872 emigrated to Romania, where he continued in journalism, working with Ion Luca Caragiale and translating from Romanian. Became something of an authority on Romania, specialising on the subject and publishing history books and a dictionary.

Gustave Hinstin (1834-94). Born Paris. Jewish origin, formerly Einstein. Ecole Normale 1853. Ecole d'Athènes 1856 (see Lespès reminiscences, Note 2) 1863-6: taught Greek, Latin and French at Pau lycée. Thesis at Sorbonne 1877. University of Dijon 1878. Wrote books on the classics, and finally teacher in Paris lycée. Léon-Paul Fargue the poet is said to have interviewed Hinstin, who had no recollection whatever of his former pupil Ducasse. (See also Lucienne Rochon, "Le Professeur de Rhétorique de Lautréamont: Gustave Hinstin", in *Europe*, Sept. 1966.)

2. Ducasse here returns to the birth of poetry, the classical tragedians and their different attitudes towards their public. Presumably the rationality of Sophocles, the moralities of Euripides, being the more impersonal, are preferred to the more specifically "religious" Aeschylus, who, as Goldfayn & Legrand (op. cit.) observe, more directly and emotionally involves the spectators: these, like his protagonists, must ultimately bow down to and accept the will of Destiny. In the light of Pierre Reverdy's remark that Lautréamont is "the only French tragic poet", perhaps *Les Chants de Maldoror* is his Aeschylean work, with Ducasse the outsider elevated to a pseudonymous aristocracy – the author-as-God, with a vengeance!

3. Maldoror-Lautréamont had "defeated" God. Hence lower case. Later Ducasse's view of and terms for the Creator change – to Elohim, capital E.

4. *Edward Young* (1681-1765). English clergyman best known for his gloomy long poem "The Complaint, or Night Thoughts on Life, Death and Immortality" (1742-45). Occasionally memorable ("procrastination is the thief of time") but mainly dull neo-Miltonic blank verse and elegiac philosophising, this poem was a precursor of the new wave of English Romanticism. Several French

translations, including Le Tourneur's, extant in France by mid-nineteenth century. Nocturnal poetry, implies Ducasse, must come into the light of day and reason.

5. Reference to sacred frenzy of Delphic oracle, said to have straddled her incense-laden tripod when prophesying. "Classical" image of "romantic" inspiration.

6. Victor Hugo published his drama *Cromwell* (1827) together with a famous preface, which became a sort of manifesto of the Romantic school in France.

Mademoiselle de Maupin (1835). Novel by Théophile Gautier (1811-72); long romance whose sensuous sexuality had caused scandal at the time. Its Preface upheld the "art for art's sake" doctrine that formal beauty and aesthetic values were what counted. By Baudelaire's and Flaubert's time beauty had come to mean perfect unity of form and content.

Dumas fils. Alexandre Dumas (1824-95), author of novel *La Dame aux Camélias* (1848; even more successful when dramatised in 1852), was given to writing Prefaces and preaching reform of evils while somewhat relishing their depiction. See also Ducasse's jibe, "thighs like camellias".

7. *Abel-François Villemain* (1790-1870). Literary critic, historian, scholar, politician. At thirty-one Member of Académie Française. Minister of Public Instruction. Died mad.

8. *Eugène Sue* (1804-75). Well-known popular author of serials and mysteries. Works include *Mysteries of Paris* (1842-3); *The Wandering Jew* (1844-5) (see Addenda, Note 42a); and of course, *Latréaumont* (1838), from which Ducasse probably took his pseudonym.

Frédéric Soulié (1800-47). One of the first successful writers of *romans-feuilletons* (serialised novels) – along with Sue, Balzac, Sand, etc. Titles include *The Memoirs of the Devil* (1837-8).

9. Back, presumably, to Marguerite Gautier – "la dame aux camélias" and courtesan.

10. Alfred de Musset (1810-57). "Rolla", his Byronic poem, was published in 1852. One of the great figures, with Hugo, Lamartine and Vigny, of the French Romantic movement.

11. Byron (1788-1824) d. Missolonghi during Greek War of Independence against the Turks.

12. *Troppmann*. See Addenda, Note 42a.

Louis-Auguste Papavoine (1783-1825). Draper who in 1824 murdered two children out walking with their mother in the Bois de Vincennes. Guillotined.

Victor Noir. Real name Yvan Salmon; opposition journalist shot dead in an argument by Prince Pierre Napoleon Bonaparte (subsequently acquitted) in 1870. Immense Republican demonstration at his funeral.

Charlotte Corday (1768-93). Stabbed the revolutionary Marat to death in his bath. Guillotined.

13. Cf. *les ficelles du roman* at the start of *Chant 6*. (*Lautréamont's Maldoror*, p.172 and Note 93, p.211.)

14. *Konrad.* Mickiewicz's hero. See Letter III, Note 6.

Manfred; Lara; The Corsair; Cain; Don Juan. All titles of poems by Byron (who is mentioned also in Letter III).

Mephistopheles, Werther, Faust. All Goethe characters.

Rodin. Hero of Sue's *The Wandering Jew* (see Note 8 above).

Caligula. Alexandre Dumas *père* published five-act verse tragedy of this name in 1837.

Cain. Hugo and Baudelaire, as well as Byron, wrote of him.

Iridion. Poem (1845) by Polish poet Krasinski (1812-59), translated into French in 1870.

Colomba. Heroine of *Prosper Mérimée* (1803-70), novelist and short-story writer with romantic-exotic bias, best known for *Carmen* (1847).

Ahriman. Principle of Evil in Zoroastrianism. Mentioned by Byron, Mickiewicz, Leconte de Lisle.

Manichean manitous. Cf. *Lautréamont's Maldoror* (pp.52-3), for vision of creator devouring blood and brains of his victims. Here in *Poésies* the evil side of gnostic/dualistic thought is rejected.

Prometheus. Shelley or Aeschylus. Both rejected for depicting in their works Man-as-Rebel against God and Order. Cf. the Titans.

15. Both Bedlam and prison. See *Lautréamont's Maldoror*, Note 20, p.207.

16. Cf. comment by Poulet-Malassis on *Les Chants de Maldoror* (p.146).

17. See Note 5.

18. *Vicomte François-René de Chateaubriand* (1768-1848). Writer, soldier, politician. A great precursor of French Romanticism. After highly active and adventurous life settled into role of grand old man of letters, editing his autobiography *Memoirs d'outre-tombe*, written between 1811 and 1841, and as its title implies, only published – purposely – after his death. Arch-egotist, with melancholy, plangently evocative style, his personal romanticism even extended to the site of his own grave, the isolated Rocher du Grand-Bé, a rocky islet off Saint-Malo.

Obermann (1804). Eponymous hero of the famous epistolary pre-Romantic novel by Senancour (1770-1846), dealing largely with melancholy and ennui. Highly influential, it is interesting to note that Senancour was himself considerably promoted by Sainte-Beuve in his weekly literary columns (*lundis*). See Letter III, Note 7. English readers in the mid-nineteenth century knew of Senancour via Arnold's poetry and prose.

Johann Paul Friedrich Richter (1763-1825). German Romantic writer, translated into French by Mme de Staël. *Flower, Fruit and Thorn Pieces* (1796) contains the dream referred to – the dead Christ. Influenced Vigny, Gautier, Nerval and many others.

Dolores de Veintemilla. Born Quito, Ecuador 1829. Poetess who committed suicide aged twenty-eight after an unhappy adulterous affair.

the Raven of Allan. Jocular reference to Edgar Allan Poe's poem. Nerval (see Note 81) is reputed to have kept a raven in romantic homage to the American writer.

the Pole's Infernal Comedy. Long poem by Krasinski (see also Note 14), translated into French in 1870.

Zorilla. Either Manuel Ruiz Zorrilla (1834-95), Spanish politician and revolutionary, exile in Paris in 1866. Or, more likely, the Spanish poet and playwright José Zorrilla y Moral (1817-93). Why the eyes of either gentleman should be particularly bloodthirsty is unclear. Valéry Larbaud suggested a possible misprint – *yeux* for *dieux*.

A Carcass. Title of poem from Baudelaire's *Les Fleurs du Mal* (1857).

the Hottentot Venus. Baudelaire's half-caste mistress, Jeanne Duval.

The familiarity of the epithets, the nicknames, the denial of surnames, together with the consistent misspellings are all part of Ducasse's technique of dismissal-through-absurdity – further proof of the power of language to be demonstrated rather differently in part II of *Poésies*.

19. Among the many meanings of *canard* are: hoax, gossip, broadsheet or rag (the last as in the twentieth-century French satirical paper *Le Canard Enchaîné*). *Canard* is also the term for a sugar lump dipped in coffee or alcohol. Caradec (op. cit.) has interestingly suggested that this complex image mirrors journalists' gatherings on the café terraces during the hours of *apéritifs*, when scurrilous stories are exchanged over drinks, later to be inserted slyly into their cynical articles. A far cry from the serious-minded Messrs Sircos and Damé whom Ducasse is here implicitly mocking.

20. *Adamastor*. The giant of the storms in the epic poem *The Lusiads* (1572) by the Portuguese writer Luís Vas de Camoës (1525-80).

Jocelyn. 1836 narrative poem by Lamartine (1790-1869), another very influential French Romantic who dealt in melancholy and who, like so many other French writers from Chateaubriand to Hugo to (more recently) Malraux, travelled adventurously and extensively, dabbled in politics and saw themselves in heroic or quasi-prophetic roles.

Rocambole. Eponymous hero of lengthy serial novel by Ponson du Terrail (see *Lautréamont's Maldoror*, Note 101, p.211), mentioned by name in *Les Chants* and greatly influencing *Chant* 6.

21. Auguste Franck (1809-93) was a highminded Sorbonne professor who wrote essays on the immortality of the soul, duty, love of God, Man, Fatherland, etc.

22. De Musset (see Note 10) published this autobiographical novel about his affair with George Sand in 1836. Gloom and disillusionment again. Ducasse no doubt implies criticism too of the Romantic artist's life — eventful, debauched, drawing its material from its own suffering and, inevitably, abbreviated.

23. Jules Lermina (1839-1915) wrote under name of William Cobb. "Les Fous" is the title of one of his fantastic stories from a collection called *Histoires Incroyables*, which the author himself stated was intended for those of nervous disposition who liked nightmares!

24. Characters in Victor Hugo's *L'Homme qui rit* (1869), a lengthy and often ludicrous novel of seventeenth-century England. Gwynplaine, his face mutilated, loves the blind girl Dea. She dies in the end and he, grief-stricken, commits suicide by drowning.

25. Théramène is the tutor and confidant of Hippolyte in Racine's *Phèdre* (1677), who, in a famous speech, returns to tell Theseus of the death of his son Hippolytus, the eponymous subject of Euripides's play on which Racine based his own.

26. Title of well-known episode in Bernardin de Saint-Pierre's *Etudes de la Nature* (1787), a romance set largely in Mauritius. Virginie, returning from France, is shipwrecked and drowns rather than strip off her clothes and accept help from a naked sailor. Paul, who has loved her since infancy, dies of a broken heart. (Cf. shipwreck scene in *Lautréamont's Maldoror*, pp.72-8.)

27. Paul Féval (1817-87). Popular and prolific author of sensational serial-novels such as *The Hunchback* (1858).

Leconte de Lisle (1818-94). Poet, leader of the Parnassian school (in many ways opposed to Romanticism), but still often a gloomy writer, and certainly in middle age a "hack", in the sense that he eked out a living through journalism, having to accept in 1864, out

of poverty, an Imperial Pension.

The Blacksmith's Strike. Title of a long, very prosaic 1869 poem by François Coppée (1842-1908), full of "worthy" sentiments by a popular if banal writer of the time. Damé's *L'Avenir* attacked both its versification and thought — slipshod and immoral in that magazine's view.

28. "Novissima verba" was Lamartine's poem from *Les Harmonies* (1830); "Ultima verba", the title of a poem from Hugo's *Les Châtiments* (1853). "Newest" words (in the sense of latest fashions) and "last" words (in the sense of definitive statements, Romantic manifestoes from the deathbed, etc.) alike held up to ridicule.

29. The village near Geneva, but just inside France, where Voltaire lived from 1758-78.

30. Note the misspellings of Chateaubriand, Senancour, etc. Half the names in the list have wrong accents or are spelt eccentrically — a characteristically sweeping Ducassian expression of humorous superiority.

Ann Ward Radcliffe (1764-1823), best known for her novels *The Mysteries of Udolpho* (1794) and *The Italian* (1797). Mrs Radcliffe, besides being very popular in her day, was and is still regarded as one of the great practitioners of the Gothic novel.

Charles Robert Maturin (1782-1824). Another great Gothic novelist, this Irish writer (whose epithet is also translatable as "Godfather-of-Gloom"), is best known for the extraordinary novel *Melmoth the Wanderer* (1820), which Ducasse undoubtedly knew and sections of which he echoed or referred to in *Les Chants* (see *Lautréamont's Maldoror*, Appendix A, p.213; also p.152 of this book).

Mikhail Lermontov (1814-41). Russian admirer of Byron. Poet and prosewriter, killed in duel. Author of the classic novel *A Hero of Our Time* (1840).

31. First mention of *Pascal*, who will play a large part in the writing of *Poésies II*. Blaise Pascal (1623-82), philosopher and physicist, was born in Clermont-Ferrand, son of a magistrate. Precocious taste for mathematics. Developed first calculating machine (1642-52). In 1654 underwent mystical experience and was converted to religious life. Took up residence in 1655 at Port-Royal, the Jansenist convent south-west of Paris at one of whose schools Racine was a pupil. He died in Paris, his general ill-health aggravated by self-mortification. Published in 1656-7 *Lettres Provinciales* (an anti-Jesuit work later placed on the Index) and in

1670 the incomplete version of the anyhow fragmentary *Pensées*, since when there have been numerous different texts of this classic work.

32. The two celebrated passages mentioned, from Musset's poems "La Nuit de Mai" (not "Rolla", as Paul Lespès states, see p.137) and "Lettre à Lamartine" respectively, Ducasse scornfully terms "cadavers".... "Hebrew verse" may be a personal remark aimed at Gustave Hinstin (see Note 1).
33. Cf. *Macbeth*, Act V, sc.1. "Out, out damned spot!" etc.
34. Cf. Vauvenargues: "Le génie garantit les facultés du coeur."

Luc de Clapiers, Marquis de Vauvenargues (1715-47), was born in Aix-en-Provence. Served in army but resigned commission in 1743. Diplomacy thereafter, but a smallpox attack ruined his health. Devoting himself to literature, he lived in poverty in Paris and died young – which links him with Ducasse, who like him was scarcely read during his lifetime and adopted a title as pseudonym. No verified likeness of either exists. Vauvenargues's *Introduction à la connaissance de l'esprit humain, suivie de réflexions et maximes* (1746) went mostly unnoticed until the nineteenth century. Where La Rochefoucauld (see Note 72 below) saw man dominated by vanity and egoism, and Pascal (see Note 31) stressed man's intellectual impotence, Vauvenargues was more optimistic. He acknowledged the presence of both good and evil in man, finding in the heart's spontaneous impulses (rather than in reason), the source of action, and in the passions (appropriately directed) the fount of moral energy.

35. Cf. Vauvenargues: "Les grandes pensées viennent du coeur."
36. Cf. Vauvenargues: "La prospérité fait peu d'amis."
37. Cf. Dante's *Inferno* III, 9: "Abandon hope, all ye who enter here." An echo, too, in the inscription over the brothel in *Les Chants* (see *Lautréamont's Maldoror*, p.101).
38. Cf. *Hamlet* I, 2: "Frailty, thy name is woman!"
39. Cf. Pascal: "J'écrirai ici mes pensées sans ordre, et non pas peut-être dans une confusion sans dessein: c'est le véritable ordre, et qui marquera toujours mon objet par le désordre même. Je ferais trop d'honneur à mon sujet, si je le traitais avec ordre, puisque je veux montrer qu'il en est incapable."
40. Cf. Pascal: "L'homme n'est qu'un roseau, le plus faible de la nature; mais c'est un roseau pensant. Il ne faut pas que l'univers entier s'arme pour l'écraser: une vapeur, une goutte d'eau suffit pour le tuer. Mais, quand l'univers l'écraserait, l'homme serait encore plus noble de ce qui le tue, parce qu'il sait qu'il meurt, et

l'avantage que l'univers a sur lui, l'univers n'en sait rien."
41. Goldfayn and Legrand, Jean and Mezei and other commentators have expounded lengthily upon Lautréamont-the-Alchemist, Ducasse-the-Cabbalist, etc. Anyone interested in such esoteric knowledge is referred to their writings. This edition of the *Poésies* is more concerned with establishing a reliable and readable English text than with the riding of favourite hobby-horses or trying to prove that Ducasse had the secret of the Philosopher's Stone. Ducasse's use here of the Hebrew word "Elohim" with its complex meanngs, its masculine-feminine plurality – "spirits" rather than "God" – may simply imply the rejection of a stereotype (the bourgeois Christian Deity) and the establishment of another kind of myth, so ambiguous that Ducasse himself can read any meaning he likes into the term, moulding it to his purpose; indeed, just like the texts he "corrects". The author, borrowing a term, and purporting to set up another kind of image of the Creator, in doing so appropriates both term and concept and becomes superior to either: once again the Author-as-God, the text infinity.
42. N.B. "à deux" – the simple duality of lovers for whom union becomes a narcissistic mirror is also rejected as romanticism, sentimentality. Hence the ensuing list of allusions: Romantick (in much the same sense as Gothick) paraphernalia!
43. *Chimène*. Heroine of Corneille's *Le Cid* (1637).
Graziella. Title of autobiographical romance by Lamartine, published in book form in 1852.
By the absurd choice of parallels Ducasse sardonically emphasises the Romantics' lack of nobility and objectivity.
44. See Contemporary Reactions, Note 4, p.147.
45. References to Chateaubriand's tomb (see also Note 18); to Musset's *Le Souvenir* which refers to his affair with George Sand at Fontainebleau; the Italian poems of Byron and Lamartine; Poe's "The Raven"; Lamartine's poem "Le Crucifix"; and Young's "Night Thoughts" (see also Note 4).
46. Cf. Vigny's "L'Esprit Pur", a poem in which poetry is called "the dove with brazen beak". Alfred de Vigny (1797-1863), perhaps because of his intellectuality one of the only Romantics spared by Ducasse. His seclusion and a certain stoicism may have been in his favour here, also the fact that he encouraged younger writers and had written stories about unrecognised genius, such as Chatterton. Anyone who withdrew from the more garish Romantic circles – as he had done – must have earned Ducasse's grudging respect.

47. Compare the witty and effective use of *détournement* and graffiti made by the Situationists and others during the *événements* of 1968. The most important and relevant Situationist of the time, Raoul Vaneigem, wrote the interesting *Isidore Ducasse et le comte de Lautréamont dans les Poésies* (*Synthèses*, numbers 150-2, 1958-9) and his best-known book, *Traité de savoir-vivre à l'usage des jeunes générations* (Paris, Gallimard, 1967; translated as *The Revolution of Everyday Life* by Paul Sieveking and John Fullerton, London, Practical Paradise Publications, 1975) is, with its abrupt transitions and caustic wit, very much influenced by Ducasse.
48. Cf. Pascal: "Si le nez de Cléopâtre eût été plus court, toute la face de la terre aurait changé."
49. Cf. Pascal: "Les belles actions cachées sont les plus estimables. Quand j'en vois quelques-unes dans l'histoire, elles me plaisent fort. Mais enfin elles n'ont pas été tout à fait cachées, puisqu'elles ont été sues; et quoiqu'on ait fait ce qu'on a pu pour les cacher, ce peu par où elles ont paru gâte tout; car c'est là le plus beau, de les avoir voulu cacher."
50. Cf. Pascal: "La grandeur de l'homme est grande en ce qu'il se connaît misérable. Un arbre ne se connaît pas misérable. C'est donc être misérable que de se connaître misérable; mais c'est être grand que de connaître qu'on est misérable. Toutes ces misères-là mêmes prouvent sa grandeur. Ce sont misères de grand seigneur, misères d'un roi dépossédé."
51. *enchaînée* – also "linked", "connected".
52. Cf. Pascal: "En écrivant ma pensée, elle m'échappe quelquefois; mais cela me fait souvenir de ma faiblesse, que j'oublie à toute heure; ce qui m'instruit autant que ma pensée oubliée, car je ne tends qu'à connaître mon néant."
53. Cf. Pascal: "Quelle chimère est-ce donc que l'homme! Quelle nouveauté, quel chaos, quel sujet de contradiction! Juge de toutes choses, imbécile, ver de terre, dépositaire du vrai, amas d'incertitude; gloire et rébus de l'univers; s'il se vante, je l'abaisse, s'il s'abaisse je le vante, et le contredis toujours, jusqu'à ce qu'il comprenne qu'il est un monstre incompréhensible."
Compare Ducasse's sardonic and surreal reworking of Pascal's last phrase.
54. Troppmann's recent murders. See Addenda, Note 42a.
55. *The Anti-Machiavel* (1740). Title of book by Frederick II of Prussia (1712-86).
56. The curious term *les cornets* implies, as Goldfayn and Legrand (op. cit.) and others have suggested, that the works of Proudhon

(1809-65), unsaleable, like Ducasse's own, were pulped – to end, literally, as "containers of reality", the grocers' paper cones wrapped around the provisions of the bourgeois! Cf. also the interlocking *cornets* in *Chant* 3 (*Lautréamont's Maldoror*, pp.101-10), that turn out to form a hair from the Creator's head.

57. *Friedrich Klopstock* (1724-1803). German poet known for his odes and for religious and patriotic dramas.

Camoes. See Note 20 on Adamastor.

58. Because one moves from philosophy in one form, Racine's, to another, Descartes's.

59. *A. Biéchy.* b. 1813. Philosophy professor and author of various books, including the one Ducasse mentions, on induction, published in Paris 1869.

Jules-Ernest Naville (1816-99). Swiss writer whose *Le Problème du Mal* was published in Geneva, 1868. See Letters, Note 10.

60. By Victor Hugo.

61. *Sauvage* – also, "savage", "wild", "uncivilised", "misanthropic".

62. *Nicholas Malebranche* (1638-1715). Theologian, scientist and philosopher. Author of many religious works, principally *La Recherche de la Vérité* (1674-5), *Traité de Morale* (1684). Admirer of Descartes, and a controversial philosopher who influenced Leibniz.

63. *De L'Intelligence* (1870), by Hippolyte Taine (1828-93). Critic, philosopher and historian and at that time professor at the Ecole des Beaux-Arts. His theory that the arts should be examined on scientific principles must have appealed to Ducasse. Highly controversial in his day, Taine influenced Zola and other contemporary writers.

64. *Gabriel-Jean-Baptiste-Ernest-Wilfrid Legouvé* (1807-1903). Novelist, Academician (1855) and playwright. Wrote *Medea* for the celebrated tragedienne Rachel, and finally won lawsuit against her when she refused to play in it. Another actress took on the role with great success, and some of his other plays also, such as *Adrienne Lecouvreur*, found popular favour. Author too of many works on family problems and relationships, topics he made something of a speciality.

Ernest Capendu (1826-68). Prolific and forgotten author of many novels popular in their day and of a great many plays.

Pierre Zaccone (1817-95). Like Capendu, prolific in the same fields of popular fiction and drama and also on occasions "ghosted" for Paul Féval (q.v.).

Father Célestin-Joseph Félix, SJ (1810-91). Published many essays and

collections of treatises on religious and educational themes.

Etienne-Paulin Gagne (1808-76). Lawyer, writer, politician. Eccentric inventor of a universal language called Gagne-monopanglotte, whose principles he published in 1845. Author of some immensely long poems, including one of 25,000 verses. Organised strange political demonstrations at which he was the only participant, and in the cause of what he called "philanthropophagy" volunteered to let himself be eaten in order to assist the starving during an Algerian famine. His offer was not, apparently, accepted.

Emile Gaboriau (1832-73). Father of French detective novel, sometimes known as the E. A. Poe of French literature. Most of his novels appeared in serial form. His famous detective Monsieur Lecoq (see novel of that title, 1869) preceded Sherlock Holmes. *L'Affaire Lerouge* (1868) is also still remembered.

Father Jean-Baptiste-Henri Lacordaire (1802-61). Entered Dominican Order of preaching friars and became one of the celebrated orators of his day. Head of famous educational college near Carcassonne. Published works included collections of funeral orations, his speciality.

Victorien Sardou (1831-1908). One of Sarah Bernhardt's favourite dramatists. Did not really come into his own as playwright until after Ducasse's death, though prolific before 1870 also. *La Tosca* (1887), *Madame Sans-Gêne* (1893).

Gustave-Francois-Xavier Delacroix de Ravignan (1795-1858). Celebrated Jesuit and preacher. Succeeded Lacordaire (see above) at Notre-Dame in 1837.

Charles Diguet (1836-18-?). Contributor to various magazines before 1870 and author of a poetry collection *Rimes de Printemps* (1861) endorsed by Lamartine. Also wrote books about hunting and shooting, and in April 1870 published – with Albert Lacroix's firm – *Les Jolies Femmes de Paris*.

65. From Corneille's drama *Cinna* (1640).
66. *Gauthier de Costes de La Calprenède* (1614-63). Author of lengthy historical novels, sometimes running to ten and twelve volumes. Also playwright.
67. *Nicolas Pradon* (1632-98). Obscure tragic poet, notorious for *Phèdre et Hippolyte* (1677), which he was persuaded by the anti-Racine cabal to write in rivalry with Racine, and which was produced two days after *Phèdre*.

Jean de Rotrou (1609-50). "Official" writer, one of the group of five under Cardinal Richelieu's direction, and known principally for *Saint-Genest* (1646) and *Venceslas* (1647).

Jean-François de Laharpe (1739-1803). Critic and dramatist. His plays are Voltairean, but it is for his more influential criticism such as *Lycée ou Cours de littérature ancienne et moderne* (1799-1805) that he is remembered, if at all.

Jean-François Marmontel (1723-99). Friend and disciple of Voltaire. Tragedian, author of novels and *Contes Moraux*, also of memoirs.

68. Faurisson (op. cit.) suggests that the dash should come after *métaphysique*, which does make more sense. Until the MSS of *Les Chants* and *Poésies* are discovered, some of these misprints and typographical oddities will remain subjects for speculation.

69. *Edouard Turquéty* (1807-67). Dull romantic poet who wrote mostly on religious themes (*Poésies Catholiques*, 1836; *Hymnes sacrées*, 1838).

70. *contenir* also in sense of "restrain".

71. Cf. Vauvenargues: "Une maxime qui a besoin de preuves, n'est pas bien rendue."

72. Cf. La Rochefoucauld: "C'est une preuve de peu d'amitié de ne s'apercevoir pas du refroidissement de celle de nos amis."

François, duc de La Rochefoucauld (1613-80). Moralist. Indulged in political intrigue against Richelieu. Wounded in Paris fighting, 1652, then lived in retirement in intellectual circles. *Mémoires* (1662); *Maximes* (1665). Bitterly pessimistic philosophy widely influential: the Jansenists approved it, seeing in it confirmation of their doctrine of the vileness of fallen Man. Voltaire (in *Candide*) was influenced by him – as he was by Pascal, in *Remarques sur les Pensées de M. Pascal*.

73. Cf. La Rochefoucauld: "Si nous n'avions point de défauts, nous ne prendrions pas tant de plaisir à en remarquer dans les autres."

74. Cf. Vauvenargues: "Nous méprisons beaucoup de choses pour ne pas nous mépriser nous-mêmes."

75. Jean Valjean, in Victor Hugo's novel *Les Misérables* (1862).

76. Reference to Lamartine's *La Chute d'un ange* (1838). An angel tries to save mankind, for love of Eve's daughter, but is himself doomed.

77. *Gustave Aimard* or *Aymard* (1818-83). Real name Olivier Gloux. Travelled widely in America; became officer in the Garde Mobile in 1848. Author of many works in the style of Fenimore Cooper, using Indians as main characters. Died mad.

Gabriel de La Landelle (1812-86). Ex-sailor, of Breton origin, wrote over sixty novels and story collections mostly on maritime themes. Knew the Corbière family well and probably influenced the poet Tristan. Contributor to the right-wing press.

78. Vauvenargues had declared that "old discoveries belong less to their original inventors than to those who put them to use." So that Ducasse here, in one of the most famous paragraphs of the *Poésies*, can refer to the precedent (should justification be required) of one of the very predecessors whose maxims he is "using"!
79. And to continue the irony, here is Ducasse's own correction/ "plagiarism" of his own alter ego, Le Comte de Lautréamont (cf. *Lautréamont's Maldoror*, page 4). No text is sacred, no words are exempt from this rigorous procedure....
80. Cf. Vauvenargues: "La raison et le sentiment se conseillent et se suppléent tour à tour. Quiconque ne consulte qu'un des deux et renonce à l'autre, se prive inconsidérément d'une partie des secours qui nous ont été accordés pour nous conduire."
81. *Gérard de Nerval* (1808-55). Pseudonym of Gérard Labrunie. One of the greatest French poets of the nineteenth century. Author of *Voyage en Orient* (1851), *Les Filles du Feu* (1854), the superb sonnets, *Les Chimères* (1854) and the extraordinary prose record of his madness, *Aurélia* (1855). His later years were spent in the shadow of insanity, and his eccentricities were legion: apart from his raven (see Note 18), and walking a lobster through the Palais-Royal gardens, he carried with him a piece of string, maintaining it was the Queen of Sheba's garter. This he is reputed to have hanged himself with, one winter night, using a railing of the Rue de la Vieille Lanterne, hence Ducasse's comment.
82. Cf. Pascal: "J'avais passé beaucoup de temps dans l'étude des sciences abstraites; mais le peu de gens avec qui on peut en communiquer m'en avait dégoûté. Quand j'ai commencé l'étude de l'homme, j'ai vu que ces sciences abstraites ne lui sont pas propres, et que je m'égarais plus de ma condition en y pénétrant que les autres en les ignorant; et je leur ai pardonné de ne point s'y appliquer. Mais j'ai cru trouver au moins bien des compagnons dans l'étude de l'homme, puisque c'est celle qui lui est propre. J'ai été trompé. Il y en a encore moins qui l'étudient que la géometrie."
83. Cf. Pascal: "Nous perdons encore la vie avec joie, pourvu qu'on en parle."
84. Cf. Victor Hugo's poem "Tristesse d'Olympio", from *Les Rayons et les Ombres* (1840).
85. *Hégésippe Moreau* (1810-38). Minor Romantic poet. Life of dissipation and increasing poverty ended in the workhouse. Author of the bitter "Ode à la faim".

Jacques-Charles-Louis de Malfilâtre (1732-67). Poet of promise who died young and unknown after considerable hardships. Gilbert

(q.v.) wrote that "hunger laid Malfilâtre unknown in his grave".

Nicholas-Joseph-Laurent Gilbert (1751-80). Farmer's son who moved to Paris. Some small measure of fame, but like the above, died young and poor. Vigny idealised him in *Stello*, a collection of stories celebrating unrecognised talents (1832).

André Chénier (1762-94). Famous part-Greek French poet, much influenced by the classics, yet paving the way for the Romantics through his metrical innovations. Long theoretical poem on the literary art, "L'Invention". Involved in early stages of French Revolution then, protesting against its excesses, was guillotined.

The group of poets mentioned above are not contrasted or compared in terms of literary merit, but mentioned together as sad examples of real or legendary "bad ends".

86. Romanticism versus Reality: writing as a conscious *act*. "The object of poetic activity is essentially language: whatever his beliefs and convictions, the poet is more concerned with words than with what these words designate." Octavio Paz's comment from his essay "What does Poetry name?" seems relevant here, and one can see why Ducasse appeals to a whole new breed of French literary critics – Pleynet, Sollers and the *Tel Quel* group.

87. N.B. *régulateur* in sense of governor/regulator for the soul's mechanism. Ducasse rather aggressively and obscurely tackles here the clash between general reason (which he approves) and individual imagination (which in the wayward self-indulgent Romantic sense he now claims to distrust). The latter, after all, is the *folle du logis* implied by the sardonic gender change in the last sentence from *régulateur* to *régulatrice*.

88. Moving again from the individual to the universal, *phénomène* also implies wonder, and freakish (hence for Ducasse "Romantic") singularity.

89. Cf. La Rochefoucauld: "L'amour de la justice n'est, en la plupart des hommes, que le crainte de souffrir l'injustice."

90. Cf. Kant's comment: "Reason does not have it that war must one day disappear, but that one must act as if war should disappear." When Ducasse's words were published, France was a month away from war with Prussia.

91. *Philippe Quinault* (1635-88). Wrote tragedies and comedies with some success prior to the rise of Racine. After 1670 wrote libretti for operas composed by Lulli. His tragedies, however, were full of verse maxims.

92. Cf. Voltaire: "Dieu a fait l'homme à son image, mais celui-ci le lui a bien rendu."

93. Cf. Pascal: "Contradiction est une mauvaise marque de vérité: plusieurs choses certaines sont contredites; plusieurs fausses passent sans contradiction. Ni la contradiction n'est marque de fausseté, ni l'incontradiction n'est marque de vérité."
94. Cf. Pascal: "C'est une chose horrible de sentir s'écouler tout ce qu'on possède."
95. Cf. Pascal: "L'homme n'est qu'un sujet plein d'erreur, naturelle et ineffaçable sans la grâce. Rien ne lui montre la vérité. Tout l'abuse; ces deux principes de vérité, la raison et les sens, outre qu'ils manquent chacun de sincérité, s'abusent réciproquement l'un l'autre. Les sens abusent la raison par de fausses apparences; et cette même piperie qu'ils apportent à la raison, ils la reçoivent d'elle à leur tour: elle s'en revanche. Les passions de l'âme troublent les sens, et leur font des impressions fausses. Ils mentent et se trompent à l'envi."
96. Most quoted paragraph from *Poésies*. Also one of the most ambiguous. It could, as Goldfayn and Legrand (op. cit.) suggest, refer to the previous paragraph and thus mean "all the senses". Back to classical balance versus individual quirks, tics – tics also implying mannerisms, tricks, singularities. Note that Racine and Corneille are not exempted – as individualists, rather than as classicists – from the list. Poetry is impersonal and thus a social duty? Is this a categorical literary neo-Marxism? Order or prescription? An attack on élites or an ideal formula for the complete annihilation of "literature"? Ends with echo of Hamlet's impatient: "Words, words, words..." (II, 2). Again, it could be a call for that poetry of the future which would impersonally deal with the Good. Surrealism took it (somewhat categorically) as a practical prescription for automatic writing, transcriptions of dream (the subconscious common to all mankind), found poems, use of *faits divers*, etc.
97. N.B. "it" referring to the nation.
98. Cf. Pascal: "Le monde juge bien des choses, car il est dans l'ignorance naturelle, qui est le vrai siège de l'homme. Les sciences ont deux extrémités qui se touchent. La première est la pure ignorance naturelle où se trouvent tous les hommes en naissant. L'autre extrémité est celle où arrivent les grandes âmes, qui, ayant parcouru tout ce que les hommes peuvent savoir, trouvent qu'ils ne savent rien, et se rencontrent en cette même ignorance d'où ils étaient partis; mais c'est une ignorance savante qui se connaît. Ceux d'entre eux, qui sont sortis de l'ignorance naturelle, et n'ont pu arriver à l'autre, ont quelque teinture de cette science suffisante,

et font les entendus. Ceux-là troublent le monde, et jugent mal de tout. Le peuple et les habiles composent le train du monde; ceux-là le méprisent et sont méprisés. Ils jugent mal de toutes choses, et le monde en juge bien."

99. First sentence sometimes attributed to La Rochefoucauld.
100. Ambiguous sentence; *se confondre* also implies mingling, "never the twain shall meet" – which thus reinforces the impersonal style Ducasse wishes to establish.
101. Logical progression from previous maxim. Goldfayn and Legrand (op. cit.) suggest that its source is Victor Hugo's poem "Booz Endormi". Ducasse not only wants to reverse the false, posturing Romantic image of Woman-on-Pedestal but to emphasise man's general freedom. Woman is only "at his feet" in relation to, as a result of, the knowledge attained in the preceding maxim.
102. *Mon enfant, ma soeur* (Baudelaire). Moreau (see Note 85) addressed his beloved as "my sister". Rotrou (see Note 67) wrote a comedy, *La Soeur* (1645).
103. Aristotelian definition of tragedy; see the *Poetics*.
104. Ducasse implies that the *new* poetics, which include "correction" as a principle, will be part of a new order, logical and therefore moral, devoid of Romantic "tics", bogus individualism, self-pitying postures, etc.
105. In the poem, *Sultan, le cheval arabe*.
106. In *Confidences* (1849) and again, word for word, in *Le Manuscrit de ma mère* (1858).
107. Axioms, theorems, mockery, brook no argument or discussion. They have the cold finality Ducasse requires.
108. Cf. Pascal: "Nous ne nous contentons pas de la vie que nous avons en nous et en notre propre être: nous voulons vivre dans l'idée des autres d'une vie imaginaire, et nous nous efforçons pour cela de paraître. Nous travaillons incessament à embellir et conserver notre être imaginaire, et négligeons le véritable. Et si nous avons ou la tranquillité, ou la générosité, ou la fidélité, nous nous empressons de le faire savoir, afin d'attacher ces vertus-là à notre autre être, et les détacherions plutôt de nous pour le joindre à l'autre; et nous serions volontiers poltrons pour acquérir la réputation d'être vaillants. Grande marque de néant de notre propre être, de n'être pas satisfait de l'un sans l'autre, et d'échanger souvent l'un pour l'autre! Car qui ne mourrait pour conserver son honneur, celui-là serait infâme."
109. Cf. Pascal: "Malgré la vue de toutes nos misères, qui nous touchent, qui nous tiennent à la gorge, nous avons un instinct que nous ne

pouvons réprimer, qui nous élève."
N.B. *élever* – also "to bring up" in the sense of education.
110. Cf. Pascal: "La nature a des perfections pour montrer qu'elle est l'image de Dieu, et des défauts, pour montrer qu'elle n'en est que l'image."
111. Cf. Pascal: "Il serait bon qu'on obéit aux lois et coutumes, parce qu'elles sont lois, et que le peuple comprit que c'est là ce qui les rend justes. Par ce moyen, on ne les quitterait jamais: au lieu que quand on fait dependre leur justice d'autre chose, il est aisé de la rendre douteuse; et voilà ce qui fait que les peuples sont sujets à se revolter."
112. Cf. Pascal: "Ceux qui sont dans le dérèglement disent à ceux qui sont dans l'ordre que ce sont eux qui s'éloignent de la nature, et ils la croient suivre: comme ceux qui sont dans un vaisseau croient que ceux qui sont au bord fuient. Le langage est pareil de tous côtés. Il faut avoir un point fixe pour en juger. Le port juge ceux qui sont dans un vaisseau; mais ou prendrons-nous un port dans la morale?"
113. Cf. Pascal: "Rien n'est plus étrange dans la nature de l'homme que les contrariétés qu'on y découvre à l'égard de toutes choses. Il est fait pour connaître la vérité: il la désire ardemment, il la cherche; et cependant, quand il tache de la saisir, il s'éblouit et se confond de telle sorte, qu'il donne sujet de lui en disputer la possession. C'est ce qui a fait naître les deux sectes de pyrrhoniens et de dogmatistes, dont les uns ont voulu ravir à l'homme toute connaissance de la vérité, et les autres tachent de la lui assurer; mais chacun avec des raisons si peu vraisemblables qu'elles augmentent la confusion et l'embarras de l'homme, lorsqu'il n'a point d'autre lumière que celle qu'il trouve dans sa nature."
114. Cf. Pascal: "Nous naissons donc injustes; car chacun tend à soi. Cela est contre tout ordre: il faut tendre au general; et la pente vers soi est le commencement de tout désordre, en guerre, en police, en économie, etc."
end of course as cessation not aim.
115. Cf. Pascal: "Les hommes n'ayant pu guérir la mort, la misère, l'ignorance, ils se sont avisés, pour se rendre heureux, de n'y point penser. C'est tout ce qu'ils ont pu inventer pour se consoler de tant de maux. Mais c'est une consolation bien misérable, puisqu'elle va non pas à guérir le mal, mais à le cacher simplement pour un peu de temps, et qu'en le cachant elle fait qu'on ne pense pas à le guérir véritablement. Ainsi, par un étrange renversement de la nature de l'homme, il se trouve que l'ennui, qui est son mal le plus sensible,

est en quelque sorte son plus grand bien, parce qu'il peut contribuer plus que toutes choses à lui faire chercher sa véritable guérison, et que le divertissement, qu'il regarde comme son plus grand bien, est en effet son plus grand mal, parce qu'il l'éloigne plus que toutes choses de chercher le remède à ses maux. Et l'un et l'autre sont une preuve admirable de la misère et la corruption de l'homme et en même temps de sa grandeur; puisque l'homme ne s'ennuie de tout, et ne cherche cette multitude d'occupations que parce qu'il a l'idée du bonheur qu'il a perdu: lequel, ne trouvant point en soi, il le cherche inutilement dans les choses extérieures, sans se pouvoir jamais contenter, parce qu'il n'est ni dans nous, ni dans les créatures, mais en Dieu seul."

116. Cf. Pascal: "La nature nous rendant toujours malheureux en tous états, nos désirs nous figurent un état heureux, parce qu'ils joignent à l'état où nous sommes les plaisirs à l'état où nous ne sommes pas; et, quand nous arriverions à ces plaisirs, nous ne serions pas heureux pour cela, parce que nous aurions d'autres desirs conformes à ce nouvel etat."

117. Cf. Pascal: "La faiblesse de la raison de l'homme paraît bien davantage en ceux qui ne la connaissent pas qu'en ceux qui la connaissent."

118. Cf. Pascal: "Nous sommes si présomptueux, que nous voudrions être connus de toute la terre, et même des gens qui viendront quand nous ne serons plus; et nous sommes si vains, que l'estime de cinq ou six personnes qui nous environnent, nous amuse et nous contente."

119. Cf. Pascal: "Peu de chose nous console parce que peu de chose nous afflige."

120. Cf. Pascal: "La vanité est si ancrée dans le coeur de l'homme, qu'un goujat, un marmiton, un crocheteur se vante et veut avoir ses admirateurs, et les plus philosophes même en veulent. Ceux qui écrivent contre la gloire veulent avoir la gloire d'avoir bien écrit; et ceux qui le lisent veulent avoir la gloire de l'avoir lu: et moi qui écris ceci, j'ai peut-être cette envie; et peut-être que ceux qui le liront l'auront aussi."

121. Cf. Pascal: "Les inventions de l'homme vont en avançant de siècle en siècle. La bonté et la malice du monde en général restent la même."

122. Cf. Pascal: "L'esprit du plus grand homme du monde n'est pas si independant qu'il ne soit sujet à être troublé par le moindre tintamarre qui se fait autour de lui. Il ne faut pas le bruit d'un canon pour empêcher ses pensées: il ne faut que le bruit d'une

girouette ou d'une poulie. Ne vous étonnez pas s'il ne raisonne pas bien à présent, une mouche bourdonne à ses oreilles: c'en est assez pour le rendre incapable de bon conseil. Si vous voulez qu'il puisse trouver la vérité, chassez cet animal qui tient sa raison en echec, et trouble cette puissante intelligence qui gouverne les villes et les royaumes."

Tintamarre ("din" or "rough music") was the name of a satirical anti-establishment magazine of cultural and social criticism, precursor of *Le Canard Enchaîné* etc. (see Note 19) and founded in 1843. Ducasse's italics make the joke at the expense of Pascal's lower case.

123. Faurisson (op. cit.) also notes that *mouche* (see Littré dictionary) is also used as abbreviation for *fine mouche* in the expression "a knowing, sly fellow", "card".

124. Cf. Pascal: "Quel pensez-vous que soit l'objet de ces gens qui jouent à la paûme avec tant d'application d'esprit et d'agitation du corps? Celui de se vanter le lendemain, avec leurs amis, qu'ils ont mieux joué qu'un autre. Voilà la source de leur attachement. Ainsi les autres suent dans leurs cabinets, pour montrer aux savants qu'ils ont résolu une question d'algèbre qui n'avait pu l'être jusqu'ici. Et tant d'autres s'exposent aux plus grands périls pour se vanter ensuite d'une place qu'ils auraient prise; aussi sottement, à mon gré. Et enfin les autres se tuent à remarquer toutes ces choses, non pas pour en devenir plus sages, mais seulement pour montrer qu'ils en connaissent la vanité: et ceux-là sont les plus sots de la bande, puisqu'ils le sont avec connaissance; au lieu qu'on peut penser des autres, qu'ils ne le seraient pas, s'ils avaient cette connaissance."

The final double negations in Ducasse's text produce a strange nonsensical "distancing" Ducasse achieves often in *Poésies*: the logical destruction of logic, or the opaque clarity of words?

125. Cf. Pascal: "L'exemple de la chasteté d'Alexandre n'a pas tant fait de continents que celui de son ivrognerie a fait d'intempérants. Il n'est pas honteux de n'être pas aussi vertueux que lui, et il semble excusable de n'être pas plus vicieux que lui. On croit n'être pas tout à fait dans les vices du commun des hommes, quand on se voit dans les vices de ces grands hommes; et cependant on ne prend pas garde qu'ils sont en cela du commun des hommes. On tient à eux par le bout par où ils tiennent au peuple; car quelque élevés qu'ils soient, si sont-ils unis aux moindres des hommes par quelque endroit. Ils ne sont pas suspendus en l'air, tout abstraits de notre société. Non, non; s'ils sont plus grands que nous, c'est qu'ils ont

la tête plus élevée; mais ils ont les pieds aussi bas que les nôtres. Ils y sont tous à même niveau, et s'appuient sur la même terre; et par cette extrémité ils sont aussi abaissés que nous, que les plus petits, que les enfants, que les bêtes."

126. One section of the Port-Royal edition of Pascal's *Pensées* was entitled: *De l'art de persuader*. This is the last Pascalian "correction". A maxim, according to Ducasse, *is*, it does not plead, nor does it hector.

127. Cf. Vauvenargues: "Le désespoir est la plus grande de nos erreurs."

128. Cf. Vauvenargues: "Lorsqu'une pensée s'offre à nous comme une profonde découverte, et que nous prenons la peine de la développer, nous trouvons souvent que c'est une vérité *qui court les rues.*"

Ducasse's emendation again upholds the principle of "correction".

129. Cf. Vauvenargues: "On ne peut être juste, si on n'est humain."

130. Cf. Vauvenargues: "Les orages de la jeunesse sont environnés de jours brillants."

131. Cf. Vauvenargues: "La conscience, l'honneur, la chasteté, l'amour et l'estime des hommes sont à prix d'argent: la libéralité multiplie les avantages des richesses."

Ducasse opposes *inconscience* (unconsciousness or ignorance) to Vauvenargues's original *conscience* (conscience, as well as consciousness), thus ironically demonstrating the flexibility and limits of language. "Corrections" are not merely a matter of substituting negative for positive and vice versa, as translators, among others, soon find out!

132. Cf. Vauvenargues: "Ceux qui manquent de probité dans les plaisirs n'en ont qu'une feinte dans les affaires: c'est la marque d'un naturel féroce, lorsque le plaisir ne rend point humain."

Comments in preceding note also applicable here. Vauvenargues's original *une feinte* being "reversed" and revised by the – in this context – strange Ducassian usage *une sincère*.

133. Cf. Vauvenargues: "La modération des grands hommes ne borne que leurs vices."

Implying that great men, ideally, have no vices (in Ducasse's version).

134. Cf. Vauvenargues: "C'est offenser quelquefois les hommes que de leur donner des louanges, parce qu'elles marquent les bornes de leur mérite; peu de gens sont assez modestes pour souffrir sans peine qu'on les apprécie."

135. Cf. Vauvenargues: "Il faut tout attendre et tout craindre du temps et des hommes."

136. Cf. Vauvenargues: "Si la gloire et si le mérite ne rendent pas les hommes heureux, ce que l'on appelle bonheur mérite-t-il leurs

regrets? Une âme un peu courageuse daignerait-elle accepter ou la fortune, ou le repos d'esprit, ou la modération, s'il fallait leur sacrifier la vigueur de ses sentiments, et abaisser l'essor de son génie?"

Note Ducasse's use of asyndeton throughout the *Poésies*. Also the latinate — hence classically impersonal, hence "good" — use of superpose as transitive verb.

137. Cf. Vauvenargues: "On méprise les grands desseins, lorsqu'on ne se sent pas capable des grands succès."

138. Cf. Vauvenargues: "La familiarité est l'apprentissage des esprits." *esprits* also implying "(great) spirits".

139. Cf. Vauvenargues: "On dit peu de choses solides, lorsqu'on cherche à en dire d'extraordinaires."

140. Truism of first sentence seems deliberately to comment on the immediately preceding "correction". The first half of the second sentence, and the link implied between *songe* (dream) and *mensonge* (lie) — much clearer in the very sound of the French, and via asyndeton — seems to have been conveniently ignored by the Surrealists, who have worshipped, plundered, and expounded these often obscure texts to instigate both dogmas and dogfights.

141. Cf. Vauvenargues: "Il ne faut pas croire aisément que ce que la nature a fait aimable soit vicieux: il n'y a point de siècle et de peuple qui n'aient établi des vertus et des vices imaginaires."

142. Cf. Vauvenargues: "On ne peut juger de la vie par une plus fausse règle que la mort."

Cf. Penultimate maxim of the *Poésies*. Yet another variation/re-working.

143. The Romantic entertainer can turn philosopher, and so much the better. But note the universality and superiority of *the* (rather than *a*) moralist, emphasised by the final exclamation mark.

144. Cf. Vauvenargues: "Qui considérera la vie d'un seul homme, y trouvera toute l'histoire du genre humain, que la science et l'expérience n'ont pu rendre bon."

145. Drama being a more social than solitary act, dramatists are superior to the Romantic lyricists with their self-indulgent interior monologues and narcissism. The latter breed do, of course, write in verse. Not so Ducasse, who after titling one prose book "Songs" now calls another, *Poésies*.

146. Cf. Vauvenargues: "Le prétexte ordinaire de ceux qui font le malheur des autres est qu'ils veulent leur bien."

147. Cf. Vauvenargues: "La générosité souffre des maux d'autrui, comme si elle en était responsable."

148. Cf. Vauvenargues: "Si l'ordre domine dans le genre humain, c'est

une preuve que la raison et la vertu y sont les plus fortes."

Reason and virtue, as constituents of order in the Ducassian scale, are its inferiors, parts of the whole.

149. Cf. Vauvenargues: "Les princes font beaucoup d'ingrats, parce qu'ils ne donnent pas tout ce qu'ils peuvent."
150. Cf. Vauvenargues: "On peut aimer de tout son coeur ceux en qui on reconnaît de grands défauts. Il y aurait de l'impertinence à croire que la perfection a seule le droit de nous plaire; nos faiblesses nous attachent quelquefois les uns aux autres autant que la pourrait faire la vertu."
151. Cf. Vauvenargues: "Si nos amis nous rendent des services, nous pensons qu'à titre d'amis, ils nous les doivent, et nous ne pensons point du tout qu'ils ne nous doivent pas leur amitié."
152. Cf. Vauvenargues: "Celui qui serait né pour obéir obéirait jusque sur le trône."
153. Cf. Vauvenargues: "Lorsque les plaisirs nous ont épuisés, nous croyons avoir épuisé les plaisirs; et nous disons que rien ne peut remplir le coeur de l'homme."
154. Cf. Vauvenargues: "Le feu, l'air, l'esprit, la lumière, tout vit par l'action; de là la communication et l'alliance de tous les êtres; de là l'unité et l'harmonie dans l'univers. Cependant cette loi de la nature, si féconde, nous trouvons que c'est un vice dans l'homme; et, parce qu'il est obligé d'y obéir, ne pouvant subsister dans le repos, nous concluons qu'il est hors de sa place."
155. Cf. Vauvenargues: "O soleil! ô pompe des cieux! qu'êtes-vous? Nous avons surpris le secret et l'ordre de vos mouvements. Dans la main de l'Etre des êtres, instruments aveugles et ressorts peut-être insensibles, le monde, sur qui vous regnez, mériterait-il nos hommages? Les revolutions des empires, la diverse face des temps, les nations qui ont dominés, et les hommes qui ont fait la destinée de ces nations mêmes, les principales opinions et les coutumes qui ont partagé la créance des peuples dans la religion, les arts, la morale et les sciences, tout cela, que peut-il paraître? Un atome presque invisible, qu'on appelle l'homme, qui rampe sur la face de la terre, et qui ne dure qu'un jour, embrasse en quelque sorte d'un coup d'oeil le spectacle de l'univers dans tous les âges."
156. Cf. Vauvenargues: "Il y a peut-être autant de vérités parmi les hommes que d'erreurs, autant de bonnes qualités que de mauvaises, autant de plaisirs que de peines; mais nous aimons à contrôler la nature humaine, pour essayer de nous élever au-dessus de notre espèce, et pour nous enrichir de la considération dont nous tâchons de la dépouiller. Nous sommes si présomptueux, que nous croyons

pouvoir séparer notre intérêt personnel de celui de l'humanité, et médire du genre humain, sans nous compromettre. Cette vanité ridicule a rempli les livres des philosophes d'invectives contre la nature. L'homme est maintenant en disgrâce chez tous ceux qui pensent, et c'est à qui le chargera de plus de vices; mais peut-être est-il sur le point de se relever et de se faire restituer toutes ses vertus."

157. Cf. La Bruyère, *Les Caractères* (Des Ouvrages de l'esprit). This work (1688) enlarged in 1694, by Jean de La Bruyère (1645-96), show him to be a somewhat pessimistic moralist whose view of his society is set down with skill, concisely and ironically.

"Tout est dit, et l'on vient trop tard depuis plus de sept mille ans qu'il y a des hommes, et qui pensent. Sur ce qui concerne les moeurs, le plus beau et le meilleur est enlevé. L'on ne fait que glaner après les anciens, et les habiles d'entre les modernes."

158. Cf. Vauvenargues: "Nous sommes susceptibles d'amitié, de justice, d'humanité, de compassion et de raison. O mes amis! qu'est-ce donc que la vertu?"

159. An "original" maxim, rare in part II of *Poésies*, hence particularly interesting to find the same insistence upon friendship as in *Les Chants de Maldoror*, in which it is one of the main themes. Cf. also the dedication to *Poésies*.

160. Cf. Vauvenargues: "Nous sommes consternés de nos rechutes, et de voir que nos malheurs même n'ont pu nous corriger de nos défauts."

161. Cf. Vauvenargues: "On ne peut juger de la vie par une plus fausse règle que la mort."

See also Note 142.

162. i.e. ellipsis.

163. Fitting that the concluding maxim is another original and a final defence of precision. No trailing away into Romantic exhibitionism and vagueness (ellipsis) but a strong end, exclamatory and unanswerable.

164. The Announcement appeared at the end of the first booklet, and the note giving Ducasse's editorial address (obligatory for this kind of publication) on the reverse title page of the second, in lieu of any dedication.

The half-plaintive, half-throwaway exhortation to a putative public is rather curious in one sense (the two sections of the *Poésies* are clearly priced at one franc each), but not in another: Ducasse had had so little success as "Lautréamont" with his previous book (see

Letters, Preface, passim), that, bearing in mind the fate of Proudhon's works (see Note 56), any interest in his own books would, at that stage, have been welcome.

Letters

À un Critique

Paris, le 9 novembre 1868

Monsieur,
Auriez-vous la bonté de faire la critique de cette brochure dans votre estimable journal. Pour des circonstances indépendantes de ma volonté, elle n'avait pu paraître au mois d'août. Elle paraît maintenant à la librairie du Petit Journal, et au passage Européen chez Weil et Bloch. Je dois publier le 2e chant à la fin de ce mois-ci chez Lacroix.
Agréez, Monsieur, mes salutations empressées.

L'Auteur

À Monsieur Darasse

22 mai 1869

Monsieur,
C'est hier même que j'ai reçu votre lettre datée du 21 mai; c'était la vôtre. Eh bien, sachez que je ne puis pas malheureusement laisser passer ainsi l'occasion de vous exprimer mes excuses. Voici pourquoi: parce que, si vous m'aviez annoncé l'autre jour, dans l'ignorance de ce qui peut arriver de fâcheux aux circonstances où ma personne est placée, que les fonds s'épuisaient, je n'aurais eu garde d'y toucher; mais certainement j'aurais éprouvé autant de

To a Critic[1]

Paris, 9 November 1868

Sir,

Would you be good enough to review this booklet in your esteemed journal. Through circumstances independent of my will, it could not come out in the month of August. It is now available at the Petit Journal bookshop and in the European arcade at Weil and Bloch's. I should be publishing the 2nd Chant at the end of this month, with Lacroix.

I am, Sir, Yours Faithfully,

The Author

To Monsieur Darasse[2]

22 May 1869

Sir,

Just yesterday I received your letter dated 21 May: it was yours. Well, you must understand that I cannot, unfortunately, let this occasion pass without sending you my apologies. This is why: because, had you informed me the other day, in ignorance of what troubles might be affecting the circumstances in which I find my own self, that the funds were running out, I would have taken care not to draw on them; but assuredly I would have been quite as happy not to write these three letters[3] as you yourself not to read

joie à ne pas vous écrire ces trois lettres que vous en auriez éprouvé vous-même à ne pas les lire. Vous avez mis en vigueur le déplorable système de méfiance prescrit vaguement par la bizarrerie de mon père; mais vous avez deviné que mon mal de tête ne m'empêche pas de considérer avec attention la difficile situation où vous a placé jusqu'ici une feuille de papier à lettre venue de l'Amérique du Sud, dont le principal défaut était le manque de clarté; car je ne mets pas en ligne de compte la malsonnance de certaines observations mélancoliques qu'on pardonne aisément à un vieillard, et qui m'ont paru, à la première lecture, avoir eu l'air de vous imposer, à l'avenir, peut-être, la nécessité de sortir de votre rôle strict de banquier, vis-à-vis d'un monsieur qui vient habiter la capitale...

... Pardon, monsieur, j'ai une prière à vous faire: si mon père vous envoyait d'autres fonds avant le 1er septembre, époque à laquelle mon corps fera une apparition devant la porte de votre banque, vous aurez la bonté de me le faire savoir? Au reste, je suis chez moi à toute heure du jour; mais vous n'auriez qu'à m'écrire un mot, et il est probable qu'alors je le recevrai presque aussitôt que la demoiselle qui tire le cordon, ou bien avant, si je me rencontre sur le vestibule...

... Et tout cela, je le répète, pour une bagatelle insignifiante de formalité! Présenter dix ongles secs au lieu de cinq, la belle affaire: après avoir réfléchi beaucoup, je confesse qu'elle m'a paru remplie d'une notable quantité d'importance nulle...

À Monsieur Verboeckhoven

Paris, 23 octobre. — *Laissez-moi d'abord vous expliquer ma situation. J'ai chanté le mal comme ont fait Misçkiéwickz, Byron, Milton, Southey, A. de Musset, Baudelaire, etc. Naturellement, j'ai*

them. You have enforced the deplorable system of distrust vaguely prescribed by my father's eccentricity; but you have guessed that my aching head does not prevent my considering attentively the difficult situation in which hitherto you have been placed by a sheet of writing paper from South America, its main shortcoming lack of clarity; for I am not taking into account the offensiveness of certain melancholy observations which one readily forgives an old man, and which appeared to me on first reading intended to impose upon you, in the future perhaps, the necessity of deviating from your clearly defined role of banker vis-à-vis a gentleman come to live in the capital...

... Pardon me, Sir, I have a request to make of you: should my father send other funds before the 1st September, at which time my body will make an appearance before your bank door, would you be kind enough to let me know? Besides, I am at home at all hours of the day; you would only have to write me the word and it is probable that I would receive it almost as soon as the young lady who opens the door,[4] or even before, if I happen to find myself in the entrance-hall...

... And all this, I repeat, for an insignificant bagatelle of formality! To present ten dry fingernails instead of five, is that all it comes to: after giving the matter much thought, I confess it looked to me full of a notable quantity of unimportance...

To Monsieur Verboeckhoven[5]

Paris, 23 October. – Let me first explain my situation to you. I have sung of evil as did Misckiéwickz,[6] Byron, Milton, Southey, A. de Musset, Baudelaire, etc. Naturally I have somewhat exaggerated the diapason so as to do something new in the way of this sublime

un peu exagéré le diapason pour faire du nouveau dans le sens de cette littérature sublime qui ne chante le désespoir que pour opprimer le lecteur, et lui faire désirer le bien comme remède. Ainsi donc, c'est toujours le bien qu'on chante en somme, seulement par une méthode plus philosophique et moins naïve que l'ancienne école, dont Victor Hugo et quelques autres sont les seuls représentants qui soient encore vivants. Vendez, je ne vous en empêche pas: que faut-il que je fasse pour cela? Faites vos conditions. Ce que je voudrais, c'est que le service de la critique soit fait aux principaux lundistes. Eux seuls jugeront en 1er et dernier ressort le commencement d'une publication que ne verra sa fin évidemment que plus tard, lorsque j'aurai vu la mienne. Ainsi donc, la morale de la fin n'est pas encore faite. Et cependant, il y a déjà une immense douleur à chaque page. Est-ce le mal, cela? Non, certes. Je vous en serai reconnaissant parce que si la critique en disait du bien, je pourrais dans les éditions suivantes retrancher quelques pièces, trop puissantes. Ainsi donc, ce que je désire avant tout, c'est être jugé par la critique, et, une fois connu, ça ira tout seul. T.A.V.

I. Ducasse
M. I. Ducasse, rue du Faubourg-Montmartre, no 32

À Monsieur Verboeckhoven[1]

Paris, 27 octobre. — J'ai parlé à Lacroix conformément à vos instructions. Il vous écrira nécessairement. Elles sont acceptées, vos propositions: le Que je vous fasse vendeur pour moi, le Quarante pour % et le 13e ex. Puisque les circonstances ont rendu l'ouvrage digne jusqu'à un certain point de figurer avantageusement dans

literature which sings of despair only to oppress the reader and make him desire the good as remedy. It is always therefore, the good one sings, in short, only by a method more philosophical and less naïve than that of the old school, of which Victor Hugo and a few others are the sole surviving representatives. Sell, I am not preventing your doing so: what must I do for that? State your terms. What I should like is that the service of criticism be made in the style of the principal *lundistes*.[7] They alone shall judge in the 1st and last resort the beginning of a publication which will only, of course, see its end much later, when I'll have seen mine. Thus the moral at the end is not yet drawn. However there is already an immense suffering on every page. Is that then evil? Of course not. I would be grateful to you, since if the critics speak well of it, I could in subsequent editions delete some passages that are too powerful. So what I desire above all is to be judged by the critics, and once known, it'll be plain sailing. T.A.V.[8]

               I. Ducasse

To Monsieur Verboeckhoven

Paris, 27 October. – I have talked to Lacroix in accordance with your instructions. He will duly be writing to you. Your propositions have been accepted: That I appoint you my vendor, the Forty per cent and the 13th copy.[9] Since circumstances have rendered the work worthy, up to a certain point, of appearing to advantage in your catalogue, I think it can be sold at a slightly higher price, I see no objection to that. Besides, on that score, minds will

votre catalogue, je crois qu'il peut se vendre un peu plus cher, je n'y vois pas d'inconvénient. Au reste, de ce côté-là, les esprits seront mieux préparés qu'en France pour savourer cette poésie de révolte. Ernest Naville (correspondant de l'Institut de France) a fait l'année dernière, en citant les philosophes et les poètes maudits, des conférences sur Le problème du mal, *à Genève et à Lausanne, qui ont dû marquer leur trace dans les esprits par un courant insensible qui va de plus en plus s'élargissant. Il les a ensuite réunies en un volume. Je lui enverrai un exemplaire. Dans les éditions suivantes, il pourra parler de moi, car je reprends avec plus de vigueur que mes prédécesseurs cette thèse étrange, et son livre, qui a paru à Paris, chez Cherbuliez le libraire, correspondant de la Suisse Romande et de la Belgique, et à Genève, dans la même librairie, me fera connaître indirectement en France. C'est une affaire de temps. Quand vous m'enverrez les exemplaires, vous m'en ferez parvenir 20, ils suffiront.*
T.A.V.

I. Ducasse

À Monsieur Verboeckhoven

Paris, 21 février 1870

Monsieur,
Auriez-vous la bonté de m'envoyer Le supplément aux poésies de Baudelaire. *Je vous envoie ci-inclus 2 f., le prix, en timbres de la poste. Pourvu que ce soit le plus tôt possible, parce que j'en aurais besoin pour un ouvrage dont je parle plus bas.*
J'ai l'honneur etc.

be better prepared than in France to savour this poetry of revolt. Ernest Naville (correspondent for the Institut de France),[10] quoting philosophers and *poètes maudits*,[11] last year gave lectures on *The Problem of Evil* at Geneva and Lausanne that must have left their mark on people's minds through an imperceptible current which goes on expanding. He has since collected them into a single volume. I shall send him a copy. In the later impressions he will be able to mention me, for I take up with more vigour than my predecessors this strange thesis and his book, which has come out in Paris with Cherbuliez the bookseller, correspondent for French Switzerland and Belgium, and at Geneva with the same firm, will make me indirectly known in France. It's a matter of time. When you send me the copies, send me 20, they'll suffice.

T.A.V.

I. Ducasse

To Monsieur Verboeckhoven

Paris, 21 February 1870

Sir,

Would you be so kind as to send me the *Supplément aux poésies de Baudelaire*?[12] I enclose 2 francs, the price, in postage stamps. I hope this is as soon as possible because I shall be needing it for a work which I discuss below.

Yours etc.

I. Ducasse
Faubourg Montmartre, 32

Lacroix a-t-il cédé l'édition ou qu'en a-t-il fait? Ou, l'avez-vous refusée? Il ne m'en a rien dit. Je ne l'ai pas vu depuis lors. — — Vous savez, j'ai renié mon passé. Je ne chante plus que l'espoir; mais, pour cela, il faut d'abord attaquer le doute de ce siècle (mélancolies, tristesses, douleurs, désespoirs, hennissements lugubres, méchancetés artificielles, orgueils puérils, malédictions cocasses, etc., etc.). Dans un ouvrage que je porterai à Lacroix aux 1ers jours de Mars, je prends à part les plus belles poésies de Lamartine, de Victor Hugo, d'Alfred de Musset, de Byron et de Baudelaire, et je les corrige dans le sens de l'espoir; j'indique comment il aurait fallu faire. J'y corrige en même temps 6 pièces des plus mauvaises de mon sacré bouquin.

À Monsieur Darasse[2]

Paris, 12 mars 1870

Monsieur,
Laissez-moi reprendre d'un peu haut. J'ai fait publier un ouvrage de poésies chez M. Lacroix (B. Montmartre, 15). Mais une fois qu'il fut imprimé, il a refusé de le faire paraître, parce que la vie y était peinte sous des couleurs trop amères, et qu'il craignait le procureur général. C'était quelque chose dans le genre de Manfred de Byron et du Konrad de Misçkiewicz, mais, cependant, bien plus terrible. L'édition avait coûté 1 200 f., dont j'avais déjà fourni 400 f. Mais, le tout est tombé dans l'eau. Cela me fit ouvrir les yeux. Je me

I. Ducasse
Faubourg-Montmartre, 32

Has Lacroix given up the edition, or what has he done with it? Or have you refused it? He has told me nothing about it. I have not seen him since then. – You know, I have disowned my past. I now sing only of hope; but for that one must first attack the doubt of this century (melancholias, sadnesses, sorrows, despairs, lugubrious whinnies, artificial mischiefs, puerile pride, comical maledictions etc., etc.). In a work I will deliver to Lacroix during the 1st days of March, I take up the most beautiful poetry of Lamartine, Victor Hugo, Alfred de Musset, Byron and Baudelaire, and correct it in the direction of hope; I outline how it ought to have been done. I am correcting at the same time 6 of the worst bits of my confounded old book.

To Monsieur Darasse[13]

Paris, 12 March 1870

Sir,

Allow me to resume from a while earlier. I have had a book of poetry published by M. Lacroix (B. Montmartre, 15). But once it was printed he refused to let it appear, because life was painted there in colours that were too bitter, and he feared the Attorney General.[14] It was something in the genre of Byron's Manfred and Mickiewicz's Konrad,[15] but far more terrible, however. Publication cost 1200 francs, of which I had already found 400. But the whole thing went down the drain. That made me open my eyes. I told my-

disais que puisque la poésie du doute (des volumes d'aujourd'hui il ne restera pas 150 pages) en arrive ainsi à un tel point de désespoir morne, et de méchanceté théorique, par conséquent, c'est qu'elle est radicalement fausse; par cette raison qu'on y discute les principes, et qu'il ne faut pas les discuter: c'est plus qu'injuste. Les gémissements poétiques de ce siècle ne sont que des sophismes hideux. Chanter l'ennui, les douleurs, les tristesses, les mélancolies, la mort, l'ombre, le sombre, etc., c'est ne vouloir, à toute force, regarder que le puéril revers des choses. Lamartine, Hugo, Musset se sont métamorphosés volontairement en femmelettes. Ce sont les Grandes-Têtes-Molles de notre époque. Toujours pleurnicher! Voilà pourquoi j'ai complètement changé de méthode, pour ne chanter exclusivement que l'espoir, l'espérance, LE CALME, le bonheur, LE DEVOIR. Et c'est ainsi que je renoue avec les Corneille et les Racine la chaîne du bon sens et du sang-froid, brusquement interrompue depuis les poseurs Voltaire et Jean-Jacques Rousseau. Mon volume ne sera terminé que dans 4 ou 5 mois. Mais, en attendant, je voudrais envoyer à mon père la préface, qui contiendra 60 pages; chez Al. Lemerre. C'est ainsi qu'il verra que je travaille, et qu'il m'enverra la somme totale du volume à imprimer plus tard.

Je viens, Monsieur, vous demander si mon père vous a dit que vous me délivrassiez de l'argent, en dehors de la pension, depuis les mois de novembre et de décembre. Et, en ce cas, il m'aurait fallu 200 fr., pour l'impression de la préface, que je pourrais envoyer, ainsi, le 22, à Montevideo. S'il n'avait rien dit, auriez-vous la bonté de me l'écrire?

J'ai l'honneur de vous saluer.

I. Ducasse
15, rue Vivienne

self that since the poetry of doubt (of today's volumes not 150 pages will remain) has reached such a point of gloomy despair and theoretical nastiness, therefore it's because it is radically false; and the reason is that *it discusses principles, and one must not discuss them*: it's more than unjust. The poetic moans of this century are only hideous sophisms. To sing of boredom, suffering, miseries, melancholias, death, darkness, the sombre, etc., is wanting at all costs to look only at the puerile reverse of things. Lamartine, Hugo, Musset have voluntarily metamorphosed into sissies. These are the Great-Soft-Heads of our epoch. Always snivelling! That is why I have completely changed method, to sing exclusively of *hope, expectation*, CALM, *happiness*, DUTY. And thus I rejoin with the Corneilles and Racines the chain of good sense and composure brusquely interrupted since the poseurs Voltaire and Jean-Jacques Rousseau. My book will not be finished for 4 or 5 months. But in the meanwhile I would like to send my father the preface, consisting of 60 pages; published by Al. Lemerre.[16] He will thus see I am working and will send me the full sum for printing the book later.

I must ask you, Sir, whether my father has instructed you to release any money to me, apart from my allowance, since the months of November and December. And in that case, I should need 200 francs to print the preface, so I could send it on the 22nd to Montevideo. If he said nothing, would you be good enough to write to me?

I am yours very truly.

I. Ducasse
15 Rue Vivienne

Notes to Letters

1. This note (or review slip) is not in Ducasse's handwriting and was found in a copy of the 1868 *Chant* 1 by Jacques Guérin and first published in the 1938 GLM edition of the *Collected Works* (Paris: introduction by André Breton). The addressee remains unknown, the signature as given. Richard Lesclide ran the *Petit Journal* bookshop and publishing firm, which specialised in – mostly anonymous – ephemera.
2. J. Darasse, 5 Rue de Lille, was banker for many French businessmen based in Uruguay and Argentina. Isidore's father, François Ducasse, was among his clients; in Montevideo Darasse had been banker to the French Consulate.

   Fragments only (not holograph) of this letter survive. They are as quoted by Léon Genonceaux in the Preface to his 1890 edition of the *Chants*. It is possible that Genonceaux himself obtained the document from Darasse's successor, Henry Dosseur.
3. Whereabouts unknown.
4. *la demoiselle qui tire le cordon*. This reference to the concierge operating the door-opening mechanism in French rented flats, usually seated in a small compartment on one side of the hall staircase and invariably elderly, formidable and Argus-eyed, may be taken as ironic by anyone who has lived in France.
5. Verboeckhoven was the associate of Albert Lacroix ("Librairie Internationale, A. Lacroix, Verboeckhoven et Cie, éditeurs à Paris, Bruxelles, Leipzig et Livourne") publishing Sue, Hugo and Zola among others. The three letters to Verboeckhoven, in Ducasse's handwriting and signed by him, were found in a copy of the *Chants* of 1869 belonging to Poulet-Malassis, publisher of Baudelaire's *Les Fleurs du Mal*. The originals are at the Doucet library in Paris.
6. *Adam Mickiewicz* (1798-1855) was a Polish poet, author of the epic poem "Pan Tadeusz", romantic dramatist, political deportee and mystic.
7. Sainte-Beuve the literary critic held Monday salons; those attending were labelled *lundistes*.
8. Abbreviation of *Tout à vous* – Yours very truly.
9. Because the *Chants* cannot safely be sold in France, Ducasse accepts that circulation may have to be restricted to Belgium and perhaps Switzerland, and that the Belgian-based firm of Lacroix, Verboeckhoven, who have after all published controversial books before are obviously better than silence. Terms quoted imply that they acquire exclusive European rights, 40 per cent discount per

copy, and every 13th copy free. Ducasse is, of course, paying to have the book printed, albeit via his father's allowance, and in so doing will provide the vanity press system with one of its few historical justifications: the production of a classic.

10. Commentators have remarked upon the rather curious logic of this letter: does it express the naïve optimism of the youthful tyro, or is it part of the further process of sophisticated clouding of issues in the cause of black humour?

Naville, a now forgotten academic, published *Le Problème du Mal* at Geneva, 1868, and in 1929 Paul Eluard, systematically trying to read all the writers mentioned by Ducasse, chanced upon a copy, of which p.180 was annotated in Ducasse's handwriting. Naville's collection of sermonising generalities seems to have been of little interest, but the Surrealists hailed the discovery – "Lautréamont's page" – with rapture.

A translation of the passages in question is given below:

ERNEST NAVILLE: THE PROBLEM OF EVIL

From: *Fourth Treatise* – "The Solution" pp.179-80 (The preceding chapter had been entitled "The primitive state of Society").

"Whom do you reckon the freer, the young tradesman who when opening his shop for the first time wonders whether to indulge in sharp practices or set up an honest business, and who has even in this hesitation the witness and consciousness of his freedom, or this same tradesman gone grey from honourable toil, chained by the repeated act of his will to the law of honour and who, feeling himself to be incapable in future of cheating, has become through the very use of his free will the servant of honour?"

Ducasse's marginal comment:

"And those who make off with the cashbox after thirty years' work? Habit is not an absolute law; after a certain time it would be negation, the actual loss of freedom."

Naville continues:

"We deem him free, in the highest sense of the word, who is free from evil."

Ducasse comments:

"Don't use this phrase, since only God is free from evil. Maybe!"

11. Walzer (op. cit.) notes that Naville's idea of "accursed poets" was scarcely Verlaine's. Corneille, Racine, Milton and Molière were among those quoted by Naville, while no section in the book dealt specifically with evil in poetry, let alone the poetry of evil.

12. *Complément aux Fleurs du Mal de Charles Baudelaire*, edn. Michel Lévy, Bruxelles, 1869. François Caradec (op. cit.) has noted that

this volume contained the poem *A une Malabaraise* and that
Ducasse in *Poésies I* refers to Baudelaire as "the morbid lover of
the Hottentot Venus."

13. Letter published in facsimile by Genonceaux in his 1890 edition
of the *Chants*. Whereabouts of the original unknown.

14. Poulet-Malassis in *Quarterly Bulletin of Publications printed
abroad and banned in France* (no.7, 25 October 1869) comments
that "the printer refused to deliver the *Chants de Maldoror* at the
moment of publication . . .". Lacroix, in difficulties over Zola's
work, had insured that his own name on the copies was followed
by the firm's *Belgian* address, Bvd. de Waterloo 42, Brussels.

15. Walzer (op. cit.) makes it clear in a note that the Konrad referred
to by Ducasse is not the eponymous protagonist of the minor
Konrad Wallenrod but the Deity-defying Konrad of the third part
of Mickiewicz's more important work, the hallucinatory epic drama
Forefathers.

16. Alphonse Lemerre, based at the Passage Choiseul, the publisher of
Frédéric Damé (q.v.), was a more sober and reassuring name to
mention to the conservative François Ducasse. It is not certain
whether Isidore Ducasse did in fact have any dealings with
Lemerre; the *Poésies* were not, of course, published by him at all,
but appeared under the aegis of Librairie Gabrie, printed by
Balitout, Questroy & Co.

Apocryphal Writings attributed to Isidore Ducasse

Things Found in a Desk

(7 November 1866)

To be possessed by a fixed idea: are you familiar with this torment?

No, your mind is too easy, your senses too cold and sedate, you don't suspect this sort of torture. Well, I am eighteen, fervent of soul, virgin in every excessive pleasure, body overflowing with life and all vigour; a fixed idea dominates me: To be free.

There's my master, my tyrant, my executioner who each day roasts me hellishly and tears at me without ever slackening grip. I'm in his hands, under his whip. I have to live, act and think like him.

Every smile, every metaphor is too feeble to make my punishment perceptible.

It's too short a chain that shackles me to the stake; it's a narrow cell around which I incessantly turn bumping against the walls.

Furthermore: it is the octopus of the novelist[1] that seizes me, holds me, grasps me in its hideous embraces. We become one: it drinks me, inhales me,[2] assimilates my being. I am no longer myself, I am it. The man is transformed; all his faculties are absorbed in the desire, it's no more than a passion served by the will.

Oh, for just a bit of liberty!

I'm hungry, give me fodder![3] An hour a day, what's that after all? Never fear, I'll do nothing more to be free, but for one hour I'll tell myself, "You can go where you wish; as fancy takes you do good or evil freely, without control,"[4] and I shall be content.

(January 1867)

Decrepit old men who in tones forlorn
Come and tell us, "Ah, I've so much to regret!"
Why lie? is it not the lycée
        For which you mourn?
Not for the dreary days nor yet
The hard taskmaster nor the beat of the drum;
But youth's brilliant years
Your heart at fifteen full of love! [5]

1868

I was young, and had deep loves, and my heart would overflow with enthusiasm!

And I mingled with the crowd, I mixed with my fellow men, speaking my thought out loud!

And they gaped back at me, without understanding.

And I withdrew from them, and they said to me: Arrogant one!

And from time to time in my solitude, my loves, my repressed enthusiasms broke out into odes, conversation; and my companions laughed and used to point me out as a madman.

So I suffered, doubted, cursed, and no one believed me sincere.

It's as if this heart, once so full of strength and love were annihilated.[6]

• • •

(*La Jeunesse*, no. 16, 12 December 1868)

Notes to Apocryphal Writings

1. "The novelistic octopus" is an equally valid alternative. As François Caradec (op. cit.) points out, this memorably Maldororian phrase reinforces the probable authenticity of this fragment. Cf. the imagery of Dazet-as-octopus in the first version of *Chant 1*, and Maldoror's copulation with the female shark, *Chant 2*.
2. Also, here in a very relevant punning sense, *aspirer* as transitive = "inspire."
3. Choice of *pâture* implies grazing and that the students are treated like cattle.
4. Also, in school context, "roll-call", "supervision", etc.
5. The original ably uses only two rhymes throughout its eight lines, but is otherwise undistinguished.
6. A dull prose-poem, its biblical "ands" starting sentences were probably clichés even then. These connected fragments are interesting however, in so far as the three-asterisk "signature", the dating and appearance of these pieces in Alfred Sircos's magazine *La Jeunesse* all suggest Ducasse's authorship, while the themes and imagery do confirm Paul Lespès's memories of Isidore Ducasse and call to mind *Les Chants de Maldoror*.

Biographical Reminiscences of Isidore Ducasse

Interview by François Alicot
Mercure de France, 1 January 1928

About "Les Chants de Maldoror" The Real Face of Isidore Ducasse

Reminiscences of Paul Lespès

M. Paul Lespès, who was his schoolfellow at the Pau lycée, has retained a very clear recollection of Isidore Ducasse. I wanted to interview him in order to add to our knowledge of the author and his intellectual development and work an almost equally clear contribution dealing with Ducasse's early background and residence in France.

"I knew Ducasse at the Pau lycée in 1864," he told me. "He was with Minvielle and me in the fifth form,[1] and in the same study. I can see him now, a tall thin young man, slightly round-shouldered, with a pale complexion, long hair falling across his forehead, his voice shrill. There was nothing attractive in his features.

He was usually cheerless and taciturn, withdrawn. Once or twice he talked to me in a lively manner about overseas countries where life was free and happy.

In the classroom he would often spend whole hours, elbows propped on his desk, head in hands, and eyes staring at a textbook he just wasn't reading; you could see he was deep in reverie. I, like my friend Minvielle, thought he was homesick and that it would be best if his parents recalled him to Montevideo.

In class he sometimes seemed keenly interested in the teaching

of Gustave Hinstin, a brilliant classics master and ex-student of the School of Athens.[2] He greatly enjoyed Racine and Corneille, and Sophocles's *Oedipus Rex* in particular. The scene where Oedipus, having finally learnt the terrible truth, utters cries of anguish and with his eyes torn out curses his destiny, seemed to him very fine. But still he regretted that Jocasta hadn't crowned the tragic horror by committing suicide on stage!

He admired Edgar Poe whose stories he had read even before admission to the school. In fact I saw him with a poetry book, Théophile Gautier's *Albertus*, which I believe Georges Minvielle passed on to him.

At school we reckoned him an odd, dreamy character, but basically a good sort, not above the average standard then, probably because of being behind with his work. One day he showed me some verses of his own. As far as I in my inexperience could judge, the rhythm seemed a bit bizarre to me and the meaning obscure.

Ducasse had a special aversion to Latin verse.

One day Hinstin made us translate into hexameters the passage about the pelican from de Musset's *Rolla*. Ducasse, who was sitting behind me on the highest bench in the class, grumbled to me in a whisper about the choice of such a subject.

The next day Hinstin compared the two best papers with those of pupils from the Lille lycée where he had recently taught classics.

Ducasse vehemently expressed his irritation:

— Why all this? he said to me. It's enough to put one off Latin.

I think there were things he didn't want to understand, so as to lose none of his aversions and his scorn.

He often complained to me of painful migraines which, as he himself recognised, were not without influence upon his mind and temperament.

At the height of summer the pupils would go swimming in the river at Bois-Louis. That was a treat for Ducasse, an excellent swimmer.

He told me one day:

– I really should cool my aching head more often in this spring water.

All these details aren't very interesting, but there is one recollection I think I should mention. In 1864, towards the end of the school year, Hinstin, who had often previously rebuked Ducasse for what he called his extravagances of thought and style, read out an essay by my schoolmate.

The first sentences, very solemn, made him laugh to begin with but soon he grew angry. Ducasse had not changed the style but weirdly exaggerated it. Never before had he given his frantic imagination such free rein. Not one sentence whose content, comprising piled-up images and incomprehensible metaphors, wasn't further obscured by verbal inventions and turns of style that didn't always conform to syntax.

Hinstin, an uncompromising classicist whose subtle critical sense never overlooked a single error of taste, took this for a sort of challenge against classical education, a bad joke at the teacher's expense. Contrary to his usual indulgence, he put Ducasse on detention. This punishment hurt our schoolfellow deeply; he complained bitterly about it to me and my friend Georges Minvielle. We did not try to make him understand that he'd greatly overstepped the mark.

Neither in the fifth nor sixth forms to my knowledge did Ducasse show any special talent for mathematics and geometry, whose enchanting beauty he enthusiastically celebrates in *Les Chants de Maldoror*. But he had a distinct liking for natural history. The animal world greatly excited his curiosity. I saw him for a long time admiring a bright red beetle which he had found in the lycée grounds during the midday break.

Knowing that Minvielle and I were shooting types born and bred, he would sometimes ask us about the habits and haunts of different Pyrenean birds and for details about their way of flight.

He had a flair for keen observation. So I wasn't surprised to read at the start of the first and fifth *Chants* the remarkable descriptions of the flight of the cranes and especially of the starlings, which he'd studied carefully.[8]

I haven't seen Ducasse again since I left school in 1865.

But a few years later in Bayonne I received *Les Chants de Maldoror*. Doubtless that was a copy of the first edition of 1868. No dedication. But the style, the strange ideas, clashing together at times as if in a free-for-all, led me to suppose that the author was none other than my former schoolfellow.

Minville told me that he too had received a copy no doubt sent by Ducasse."

I asked M. Lespès if *Les Chants de Maldoror* weren't partly the product of a wish to play a schoolboy prank, if they were not a hoax.

"I don't think so," he replied.

"At school Ducasse saw more of me and Georges Minvielle than of other pupils. Yet his stand-offish attitude, if I may use this phrase, a sort of heavy condescension and a tendency to consider himself a being apart, the obscure questions he would fire at us point-blank and by which we were completely embarrassed, his ideas, his extravagance of style which our excellent teacher Hinstin used to single out, and lastly the irritation he sometimes displayed without due cause, all these eccentricities led us to believe that he wasn't quite right in the head.

His own brand of madness revealed itself definitively in a French essay in which with a dreadful profusion of adjectives he'd seized the opportunity of accumulating the most horrible images of death. It was nothing but broken bones, entrails hanging out, bleeding or mangled flesh. It was the memory of this composition some years later that made me recognise the author of *Les Chants de Maldoror* although Ducasse had never mentioned any poetic inclinations to me.[4]

Minvielle and I, and other schoolfriends too, were sure Hinstin was wrong to put Ducasse on detention for his essay.

It wasn't a silly joke at the teacher's expense. Ducasse was deeply hurt by Hinstin's reproaches and this punishment. I believe he was convinced he had written an excellent essay full of original ideas and fine turns of phrase. Of course if you set *Les Chants de Maldoror* beside the *Poésies*, you might infer that Ducasse hasn't been sincere. But if as I believe, he was sincere at school, why not later, when striving to become a prose poet, and when in a sort of

imaginative delirium he persuaded himself perhaps that through the image of relish for the horrible he might lead souls deterred from virtue and hope back toward the good?

At school we thought Ducasse a good fellow but a little, how shall I say, cracked. He wasn't without morals; there was nothing sadistic about him.

I well remember the humorous opinion held by my friend Georges Minvielle, a very witty, pleasant man, himself something of a poet; we had each received a copy of the first edition of *Maldoror*. 'Remember that essay of his?' he said. 'He had a screw loose but now it's a lot looser!!!' "

For M. Lespès and Georges Minvielle – who died at Pau in 1923 – Ducasse's imagination and originality of style were due to a peculiar mental disposition.

To M. Lespès it's not hard to discern Ducasse's influences. These are, apart from the classics and Gautier as mentioned, Shakespeare, Shelley "whom he enjoyed" (for Ducasse spoke English well and probably, like all South Americans, Spanish), and especially Byron, certainly his greatest inspiration.

"Do you think," I asked M. Lespès finally, "that as M. Soupault says in the preface to the latest edition of *Maldoror* there may be a likeness between your schoolmate and the revolutionary agitator depicted by Jules Vallès in *The Insurgent*?"[5]

"All I can say to that is that the Ducasse I knew used to express himself with difficulty more often than not and sometimes with a sort of nervous rapidity.

He definitely was no orator capable of rousing the masses, and never at school talked politics and social revolution.

Vallès's picture of the agitator Ducasse doesn't seem to me a perfect resemblance although it does recall some of my schoolfellow's physical characteristics. The latter did not splay out his arms and legs, and his hair was brown rather than red.

That's a far cry from the orator who 'gravely climbed the steps of the dais, rolling his eyes, knitting his brows, *the three saffron wisps of his goatee* alertly bristling . . .'."

Lacroix, the publisher of *Les Chants de Maldoror*, had pre-

viously described him thus:

"He was a tall beardless young man,[6] nervous, neat and hard-working."

M. Lespès confirms the accuracy of this description.

We may thus conclude:

(1) Ducasse-Lautréamont has nothing in common with the agitator who, according to a quite usual pattern, ended up chairman of the Consistory of the Evangelical Church of Brussels;

(2) Isidore Ducasse is no fiction;

(3) *Les Chants de Maldoror* is a genuine work. Painful fruit of an excitable mind full of sombre images, M. Lespès told me.

Notes to Interview

1. *Classe de Rhétorique*. No real equivalent in British terms: an Upper Fifth or Lower Sixth, specialising in Classics, is perhaps the nearest approximation, the lycée itself being a kind of high or grammar school.
2. *Collège d'Athènes*. Two Ecoles Françaises d'Archéologie were founded in 1846, one in Athens, the other in Rome, for post-graduate Classical studies.
3. Ironically as Maurice Viroux and others have shown, both these passages were adapted/plagiarised from Dr Chenu's *Encylopaedia of Natural History* and perhaps, less obviously, from Dante's *Inferno* too.
4. Seemingly a contradiction of Lespès's earlier comment?
5. Jules Vallès (1832-85) Journalist and novelist of peasant stock and revolutionary views. Imprisoned 1853 and exiled (1871-80) for his part in the Commune. *L'Insurgé* (published 1886) is the last of an autobiographical trilogy.
6. *jeune homme imberbe* – also, "raw" or "callow" youth.

2

Extract from Preface written by Léon Genonceaux to his publishing house's edition of *Les Chants de Maldoror* (1890). The Preface contains various factual errors concerning Ducasse's date of birth, the cause of his death, etc. It should thus be read with some scepticism. But the Preface was dedicated to Genonceaux's friend Albert Lacroix, Ducasse's first publisher over twenty years previously, and it is possible that some of the following information came from Lacroix himself (cf. p.143): Genonceaux and Ducasse never met.

"He was a tall young man with brown hair, cleanshaven, highly-strung, tidy and industrious. He wrote only at night, seated at his piano. He used to declaim, would coin his phrases hammering out his tirades with the chords. This method of composition was the despair of the hotel's occupants who, often woken with a start, could have had no idea that an astonishing musician of the word, a rare symphonist of the sentence, was searching, by hitting his keyboard, for the rhythms of his literary orchestration."

3

Extracts from an article on Ducasse by Edmundo Montagne in *El Hogar* (Buenos Aires) dated 20 November 1925. This article, now virtually unobtainable, was partially translated into French and quoted from by Francisco Contreras in his *Mercure de France* article of 15 July 1927. The relevant sections, reprinted by Caradec, Faurisson and others, concern the recollections of Prudencio Montagne, Edmundo's uncle, who undoubtedly did know Ducasse. In a letter to his nephew Prudencio Montagne points out that his memories date back to the years between six and nine. Hence we must accept these tantalising fragments also with some caution for

what they are, the fruits of hindsight filtered through an old man's memory and translated from Spanish to French to English! As it is, there are three different French versions (by Contreras, A. Rodriguez and R. Lefeuvre) of some key sentences – presented here in that order.

   a. "Isidore was a young lad (at that time we were youngsters up to twenty), handsome, but extremely precocious, boisterous, insufferable."
   b. "Isidore was a nice kid (at that time we were still kids at twenty), but extremely dissolute, noisy and aggravating. No one ever mentioned his literary works to me."
   c. "He was a goodlooking fellow, mischievous, persuasive and provoking."

On Sundays, Prudencio Montagne's father and Ducasse's father would go for a walk together: "Isidore did not accompany us. Perhaps he was at school, or his father would not let him go out, fearing the tricks he could get up to in the streets. Or perhaps M. Ducasse had sent him to France for his studies. These walks lasted until 1867, the time when Isidore was in Paris."

Montagne points out that he had known Isidore "since 1864, when he was eighteen, that is," and that he continued to be good friends with François Ducasse until the latter's death. He concludes: "I heard no mention of the *Chants*, neither then nor when I grew up. All Ducasse told me, one day, post-1875, was that Isidore had died in '70. I had always thought he'd been killed in the war." [i.e. Franco-Prussian War.]

Note

For further, previously unpublished reminiscences of Isidore Ducasse, see Alvaro Guillot-Muñoz's extraordinary little book *Lautréamont à Montevideo* (*La Quinzaine Littéraire*, 1972). It is, of course, no longer possible to verify many of the anecdotes so assiduously

collected, and Guillot-Muñoz and the majority of his interviewees (mostly elderly, to say the least, at the time of interview) are now dead. The Ducasse legend lives on, however, at its most enthralling when various testimonies (notably those of Plantet and Cazeaux) converge. Subject to the above reservations, the book is highly recommended to all those interested in the childhood, adolescence, and general family background of an enigma.

Contemporary Reactions to Lautréamont

The First Review

There were no contemporary reviews of the *Poésies*. This, the first and only contemporary critical article on *Les Chants de Maldoror* – and then only of *Chant 1* in its original form, separately published – appeared in *La Jeunesse* (1st yr, No. 5, 1-15 September 1868).

LES CHANTS DE MALDOROR by * * *[1]

The first effect produced by reading this book is of astonishment: the hyperbolic bombast of the style, the savage strangeness, the desperate vigour of conception, the contrast of this impassioned language with the dullest lucubrations of our time, at first cast the mind into a deep amazement.

Alfred de Musset mentions somewhere what he calls "the Sickness of the Century": it is uncertainty about the future, contempt for the past, or incredulity and despair. Maldoror is stricken with this malady; sceptical, he grows wicked, and turns all the powers of his genius towards cruelty. Cousin to *Childe Harold* and *Faust*, he knows men and despises them. Envy eats him up, and his heart, always empty, incessantly excites itself with gloomy thoughts without ever being able to attain that vague and ideal objective he seeks and guesses at.

We will not carry the criticism of this book any further. It should be read, to feel the powerful inspiration animating it, the dark despair diffused within these lugubrious pages. Despite its faults, which are numerous, the incorrectness of style, the disorder of the scenes, we think this work will not

be mistaken for other current publications: its uncommon originality assures us of that.

EPISTEMON[2]

Other Mentions of Lautréamont

Auguste Poulet-Malassis (see Letters, Notes 5 and 14), friend and publisher of Baudelaire, had been exiled in Brussels since 1863. He made the following brief comment in his *Bulletin trimestriel des Publications défendues en France, imprimées à l'Etranger*, dated 25 October 1869:[3]

"There are no Manichees," said Pangloss. "There is myself," replied Martin. The author of this book is of no less rare a breed. Like Baudelaire, like Flaubert, he believes that the aesthetic expression of evil implies the most vital appreciation of good, the highest morality. M. Isidore Ducasse (we were curious to know his name) was wrong not to have had *Les Chants de Maldoror* printed in France. He would not have escaped the sacrament of the sixth chamber.[4]

NB. The printer refused, at the moment of publication, to deliver *Les Chants de Maldoror*, advertised as No.10 in the current Bulletin.

Extract from
p.82 of *Bulletin du Bibliophile et du Bibliothécaire*,
issue of May 1870
(This was a monthly published by Léon Techener)

"This volume, printed in Brussels, was published, we are informed, in a small edition and then suppressed by the author,

who has disguised his real name under a pseudonym. It will find a place among the bibliographical curiosities, no preface, a series of visions and reflections in bizarre style, a sort of Apocalypse whose meaning it would be futile to guess. Is it some sort of wager? The writer seems very serious and nothing is more lugubrious than the scenes he presents to his readers' eyes. We mention this strange work because it will doubtless remain unknown in France."

A brief advertisement for the book also appeared in Evariste Carrance's anthology *Fleurs et Fruits* (4th series, January 1870) – and that, as regards the book's original appearance, was that.

Notes to Contemporary Reactions

1. The author's name did not appear at all, simply the asterisks.
2. Pseudonym of Alfred Sircos, the magazine's editor and one of the dedicatees of the *Poésies* (q.v., Note 1).
3. The above appeared in Issue 7. Publication of the *Bulletin* (subscription 4 francs per annum) had begun at the start of August 1867 and would continue until the end of December 1869. Poulet-Malassis had announced that anything that attacked the Emperor or prevailing morality would be extolled in its pages.
4. Of the Tribunal de la Seine, presumably. (The Court of Cassation, for example, had five chambers.) Poulet-Malassis could have been implying here, with some justification for the bitterness, that the *chambre ardente*, the sinister special tribunal founded in the 16th century to deal in secret session with such offences as heresy, might well be revived during the latter days of the Second Empire. The courtroom, darkened, and lit only by candles and torches, whether or not the case was being heard by day or night, would have presented a tableau worthy of Maldoror himself. See also *Poésies* II, Note 44.

Additional Bibliography

My annotated centenary edition of *Les Chants de Maldoror* (LAUTRÉAMONT'S *MALDOROR*, London, Allison & Busby, 1970; New York, Thos. Y. Crowell, 1972) included a Select Bibliography, slightly expanded for the later US edition. With the appearance of what is in effect the second and final volume of Lautréamont's Complete Works, it now seems useful and appropriate to update these lists, mentioning (as before) that only some of the more recent of the numerous French editions and critical writings are included here, and that the fullest available bibliographies are still those to be found in *Oeuvres Complètes*, edited by Pierre-Olivier Walzer, Paris, Bibliothèque de la Pléiade, Editions Gallimard, 1970; and in the de Haes book and the special issue of *Entretiens* (see below).

In English
Critical
Books

Alquié, Ferdinand: *The Philosophy of Surrealism* (University of
   Michigan, 1965).
De Jonge, Alex: *Nightmare Culture* (London, Secker & Warburg, 1973).
Maritain, Jacques: *Creative Intuition in Art and Poetry* (London, Harvill
   Press, 1954).

De Jonge's book is (with Peter W. Nesselroth's excellent
Lautréamont's Imagery, A Stylistic Approach, Geneva, Librairie Droz,
1969) the only full-length study in English of Lautréamont's work.
Concentrating on the *Chants*, De Jonge's book contains some interesting
insights but too many misprints, factual errors and dubious
generalisations. A stimulating, if Procrustean, attempt to "popularise"
Lautréamont, if by no means the last or (as the publishers ludicrously
claim) the first word on the subject.

In French
Editions of Lautréamont

Oeuvres Complètes. Edited by Philippe Sellier. Paris, Bordas, 1970.
Oeuvres Complètes. Edited by Marcel Jean and Arpad Mezei. Paris, Eric Losfeld, 1971.
Oeuvres Complètes. Preface by J. M. G. Le Clézio. Edited by Hubert Juin. Paris, NRF Gallimard, 1973.

The Hubert Juin edition is particularly recommended for its informative notes, which is more than can be said for the edition concocted by those wouldbe psychoanalysts, proprietors and indeed inventors of Lautréamont, Messrs Jean & Mezei, who serve up the same unlikely conjectural brew as before.

Critical
Books

Bouché, Claude: *Lautréamont du lieu commun à la parodie.* Paris, Librairie Larousse, 1974.
De Haes, Frans: *Images de Lautréamont.* Gembloux, Ed. J. Duculot, 1970.
Faurisson, Robert: *A-t-on lu Lautréamont?* Paris, NRF Gallimard, 1972.
Guillot-Muñoz, Alvaro: *Lautréamont à Montevideo.* Paris, La Quinzaine Littéraire, 1972.
Montal, Robert: *Lautréamont.* Paris, Editions Universitaires, 1973.
Perrone-Moisés, Leyla: *Les Chants de Maldoror de Lautréamont.* Paris, Hachette, 1975.
Philip, Michel: *Lectures de Lautréamont.* Paris, Librairie Armand Colin, 1971.
Rochon, Lucienne: *Lautréamont et le style homérique.* Paris, Editions ALM No.123, 1971.
Rochon, Lucienne (et al.): *Quatre Lectures de Lautréamont.* Paris, Nizet, 1972.

Of the above selection, the books by Bouché, De Haes, Guillot-Muñoz and Philip are especially illuminating. Bouché in particular is masterly, and includes a fiercely witty and well-justified demolition of the absurdly inflated Faurisson book.

Critical

Books dealing in part with Lautréamont

Drieu la Rochelle, Pierre: *Notes pour comprendre le siècle*. Paris, Gallimard, 1941.

Weber, Jean-Paul: *Domaines thématiques*. Paris, Gallimard, 1963.

Magazines and miscellanea

Entretiens, Lautréamont issue, No.30, Spring 1971.

An admirable 240 pp. compilation edited by Max Chaleil for Editions Subervie, containing a reprint of the 1925 *Disque Vert* special issue on Lautréamont, together with much new material and illustrations.

Addenda

to the 1970 Allison & Busby edition of
Lautréamont's Maldoror

Additional Notes

Page 95 line 14. Note after *The Wandering Jew*, as follows:
42a The second section of *Chant* 2, pp.35-8, was inspired by an episode in Sue's *The Wandering Jew* (1844-5). By curious coincidence this book was the sole reading matter of the young mass-murderer Jean-Baptiste Troppmann (see *Poésies*, Note 12). Troppman, sadistic *al fresco* slaughterer of a family of eight, was guillotined in Paris on 19 January 1870, aged twenty. Lautréamont, who made use of *faits-divers*, in his fictional description of the young girl's savage mutilation preceded Troppmann's actual deeds by only a few months.

Page 115 line 6. Note after *fig!* as follows:
42b Cf. "Even as *Philemon* a Comick Poet died with extreme laughter at the conceit of seeing an asse eate figs: so have the *Italians* no such sport, as to see poore English asses, how soberlie they swallow Spanish figges, devoure anie hooke baited for them." (Thomas Nashe, *The Unfortunate Traveller*, 1594.)

Page 164 line 4. Note after *spider* as follows:
85a Cf. the spider in the opening lines of Hazlitt's famous essay "On the Pleasure of Hating" (1826), a piece with which Lautréamont may have been familiar.

Page 169 lines 3 & 4. These should now read:
The flight of the lantern-fly[89]
and Note 89 should now read:
Bichitos de luz, a species of fire-fly found in Latin

                        America. See Note 49.
Page 175 line 15.   Note after *Peking* as follows:
                        100a   Pun on *en pékin*, slang for "in mufti".

                        Addendum to Appendix A:
                        Maldoror and Melmoth

Page 213   Add to existing notes referring to Chapters IX and
                        XX the following:
                        Chapter XX.   Isidora's swoon and revival probably
                        P.257   influenced the treatment of
                                      Mervyn's. Cf. *Maldoror* pp.180-82.

Errata

Page 1, line 3: For *sudden* read *abrupt*
Page 1, line 8: For *No good for* read *It would not be good for*
Page 10, line 12: For *out of* read *from*
Page 31, line 18: delete *miss*
Page 44, line 3: For *Oh* read *Ah*
Page 91, lines 19-20: For *An unknown person* read *A stranger*
Page 95, line 3: For *unknown* read *stranger*
Page 113, line 9: For *possible* read *impossible*
Page 126, line 2: Read *of a fantastic* (incorrect spacing)
Page 174, line 32: delete *crusty*
Page 209, line 1: For *fulgorous glow* read *lantern*